I0616338

THE WILDCARD WORKBOOK

A PRACTICAL GUIDE FOR JOKERING FORUM THEATRE

By Theatre of the Oppressed NYC Facilitators
Sulu LeoNimm, Liz Morgan, & Katy Rubin

ISBN 979-8-218-02575-5

Copyright © 2022 by *Theatre of the Oppressed NYC*

CONTENTS

INTRODUCTION

THEATRE OF THE WHAT?

WHAT DOES T.O. LOOK LIKE?

When you see the word *theatre,* something pretty concrete probably comes to mind: actors on a stage, acting out a story. And when the show's over, there's an applause and then the audience goes home.

But what if the play was acted out by the people who experienced injustice in real life? What if the actors and audience could shape parts of the story together? This practice of using theatre as a tool for social change is called Theatre of the Oppressed (T.O.).

We define *oppression* as a person or a community being exploited or blocked from their own human rights, including the right to express their own identity

You might've already guessed that this looks pretty different than most professional theatre. Originally created in the 1960s by Brazilian playwright and activist Augusto Boal, Theatre of the Oppressed uses a range of Games and exercises to bring communities together and tell their stories. In T.O., stories about challenging injustice and oppression are developed and performed by the people who experience them.

Boal borrowed many of his ideas from his colleague Paulo Freire, who wrote *Pedagogy of the Oppressed.* In Freire's practice of "problem-posing" education, learners critically engage with real-world issues as they work toward liberation. You may understand T.O. better by reading some of Freire's work.

During each performance, actors and audiences collaborate to think critically about the social justice problems posed in the play and brainstorm possible resolutions together. The goal is to inspire transformative action in the real world by breaking from the traditional understanding of professional theatre and inviting audiences to participate.

T.O. is practiced around the world as a powerful tool for activism, community building, and creative expression. Theatre of the Oppressed NYC (TONYC), is a New York City-based company that uses T.O. techniques in partnership with communities facing discrimination to form theatre troupes. These troupes create and perform plays based on their own experiences as a way to challenge injustice.

This workbook is an introduction to the ways that TONYC has applied Theatre of the Oppressed practices to make change together with our local communities.

While there are many practices that make up Theatre of the Oppressed, TONYC mostly focuses on one called Forum Theatre.

Forum Theatre looks something like this:

Forum Theatre is the process of developing an original play (called a Forum Play) by a troupe of actors working together. This usually looks like scenes that show a problem caused by oppression that the actors are facing.

Once the scene is finished, the audience is invited to step into the play and improvise possible ways to address this problem. This is called an Intervention.

The actors in the play improvise responses to the audience (who are now called Spect-Actors, because they're now a part of the play).

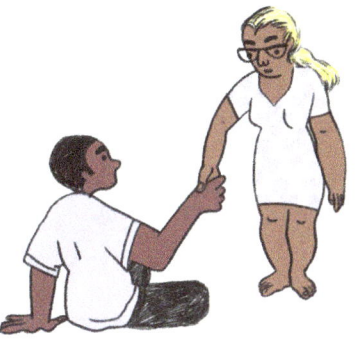

All of this is facilitated by someone called a Joker. Unlike traditional theatre, T.O. isn't led by a director.

Instead, T.O. comes to life through a facilitation style called "Jokering." Jokering is a practice of designing exercises and experiences that lead to a deeper understanding of the world.

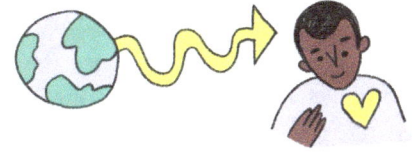

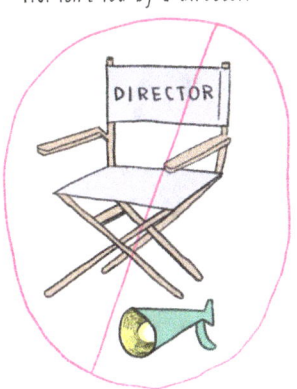

Jokering involves asking questions that move us all from oppression to liberation. (This workbook is unofficially called "How to be a Joker"!)

Before we get too far, we want to explicitly challenge some of the expectations about the rehearsal and performance processes of "professional" or "traditional" theatre. While most of theatre-making as we know it offers the audience a final product, T.O. offers the audience a *process*.

To make sure everyone can participate, TONYC has adopted inclusive practices to help make a rehearsal space that responds to people's varied needs. Here are some ways that T.O.-making looks different than professional theatre-making:

EXPECTATIONS OF WHAT A TYPICAL THEATRE PROCESS LOOKS LIKE...

OUR FORUM THEATRE REHEARSALS LOOK LIKE...

Actors act out the playwright's version of the story.

The troupe has many versions of the story and needs to agree on which version they want to show.

Actors will do whatever it takes to prepare for and perform the role.

Community members have the right to question or opt out of any activity that doesn't feel like a fit for them.

The director tells everyone else what to change.

The troupe makes decisions together, facilitated by the Joker.

The actor owns their role.

Actors may change roles to support each other and the play. Maybe this happens because someone has an important appointment, or because someone needs to tap out of playing a particular role.

The troupe doesn't talk to the audience about what they think.

The troupe prepares to hear from the audience during the show. We are ready to welcome in ideas to challenge oppressive systems and to make change.

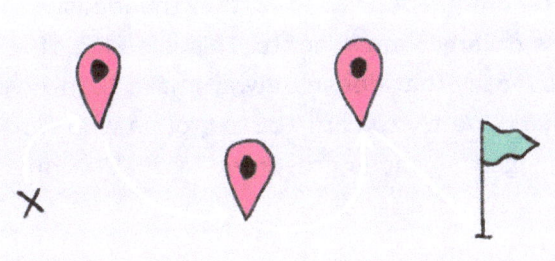

The troupe rehearses and sets every moment following the script.

We establish plot points, key words, and actions to perform. We rehearse improv so that everyone is ready for improvising with the audience.

The schedule is set and everyone arrives on time for every rehearsal and show.

Someone is late or absent, probably because of work, family, appointments, trains, or the police.

THE REAL-WORLD IMPACTS OF T.O.

Every step of the T.O. process aims to generate concrete actions that contribute to larger social movements. Here are some ways our community of actors, Jokers, and Spect-Actors have brought actions from the stage to everyday lives:

* An actor reflects on how he has never spoken to a government representative before, so he tries to make change by calling his councilmember about a housing issue.
* A Spect-Actor notices that she trusts a teacher's complaints more than her children's, and decides to pay more attention the next time her child talks about problems at school.
* A formerly incarcerated Joker reflects on how their harsh self-judgments sound a lot like oppressive statements they have heard about incarcerated folks the first time they talked to a therapist about these thoughts.

We know that plays alone aren't enough to make systemic change. Our practice at its best uses the tools and techniques of T.O. to further the ideas and actions of larger movements. This is a kind of creative advocacy that doesn't always have to involve policy makers! We try to connect to groups who work daily to change the issues presented in our Forum Plays.

Some of our favorite memories of TONYC using Theatre of the Oppressed for direct action and creative advocacy include:

Cuomoville. In 2017, TONYC was invited to work with community organizers protesting Governor Cuomo's housing policies. The troupe joined a sleepout inside of a police barricade at Cuomo's office, and performed a scene that showed the impact of his policies on the housing crisis.

UBI March. In 2019, TONYC's Rapid Response troupe, which was designed to collaborate on creative advocacy events, partnered with organizers fighting for Universal Basic Income. They kicked off the march by playing T.O. Games and making signs. And at the end of the march, they performed a scene, inviting onlookers and protestors to consider how Universal Basic Income would have impacted the main characters.

Dignity in Schools Teach-in. In 2020, the Dignity in Schools Coalition (DSC) was considering joining the Department of Education's task force to address school safety issues. Four TONYC Jokers led a DSC meeting in a decision-making process. It began with members of the coalition creating Forum scenes about the problems with school safety as well as the issues that come up working inside and outside the system.

T.O. for the (policy) win! There's often a gap between actions that individuals can take and the rules and policies that need to change to bring about justice and equity. Sometimes we move beyond Forum Theatre to engage in a T.O. technique called Legislative Theatre. At TONYC, we're experimenting with how Legislative Theatre can lead to concrete policy wins. Here's what we've been up to so far:

* After watching a TONYC performance about a transgender woman who is arrested because the police accuse her of holding fake identification, Councilmember Carlos Menchaca adapted his NYC Municipal ID bill to allow New Yorkers to name their gender or opt out of identifying their gender on their ID entirely.
* Councilmember Jimmy Van Bramer attended a performance about transphobic abuse and stated publicly that this performance inspired him to vote for the Community Safety Act.

In section 8, p. 130, you can find more of our techniques for Legislative Theatre, but most of this book is about learning to facilitate Forum Theatre. If changing the law feels too overwhelming, remember no Intervention is too small. The experiences of building, rehearsing, and performing Forum Theatre can and should catalyze direct and ethical transformations to the status quo.

What's this book all about?
This book is an introduction to Forum Theatre and the way that TONYC has applied T.O. practices to make change in our communities. It's not a nonprofit management guide or an academic textbook. This workbook is for anyone interested in using theatre as a tool for social change.

If these ideas are totally new to you, welcome! We're so glad you're here!

If you're familiar with this work and are here to sharpen your facilitation skills, feel free to skip around. This guide includes tools and reflections from Theatre of the Oppressed practitioners, but we know they aren't "one-size fits all."

These perspectives come from our specific experiences practicing this work in NYC and, since T.O. is a global practice, our views may conflict with the realities and contexts of other practitioners. We invite you to be in dialogue with our experiences and your own.

The content that follows is TONYC's attempt at posing questions that prompt a more ethical, joyful, and radical practice of Theatre of the Oppressed. This book is meant to accompany in-person, Theatre of the Oppressed trainings. We hope this book supports you in developing a Joker practice that works for you and the communities you collaborate with, and encourages you to bring your own experiences, styles, and flair to the practice.

Notes

These pages are yours! Feel free to skip around, write in the margins, rip out pages, and add your own ideas!

WHAT'S THEATRE OF THE OPPRESSED?

Whether you're new to the idea of Theatre of the Oppressed, or you're already a practitioner looking to brush up on your technique, we hope this workbook gets you excited about using theatre as a tool for sparking collective action!

Chapters 1–3 provide an overview of Theatre of the Oppressed and some of the main ideas and practices.

1. WHAT'S FORUM THEATRE?
2. WHAT'S A JOKER?
3. THE TECHNIQUES WE USE

WHAT'S FORUM THEATRE?

Chapter 1 covers all you need
to know about Forum Theatre,
including how to decide when
Forum Theatre is appropriate and
ethical for your group.

REHEARSAL FOR THE REVOLUTION

Boal sometimes called Forum Theatre a "rehearsal for the revolution."

In Forum Theatre, the Joker leads actors and Spect-Actors in creative problem-solving strategies that can be used to fight back against real-world oppressions. The final Forum Theatre performance prepares everyone in attendance to take action in real life.

The word *revolution* has a double meaning. While *revolution* refers to the new systems we dream of creating, Forum Theatre is also in a revolution—or a cycle—with our real lives. Our real lives inspire the story of our Forum Play, and the Interventions we create inspire how we might interact with systems of oppression once we leave the theatre.

NOTHING ABOUT US, WITHOUT US!

As T.O.'s origin story goes, Boal and his company of actors performed a play to an audience of farmworkers about the plight of Brazilian farmworkers whose land had been stolen by the dictatorship. The play ended with a scene where the actors playing farmers forcibly reclaimed their land. The farmworkers in the audience leapt to their feet, cheering, "Bravo! Let's do it right now!" The actors were forced to admit that they had no intention of taking part in a revolt. So, the farmworkers demanded that the actors pack up and leave. How could these actors, who had no experience with farming stolen land, encourage the workers to put their lives at risk, when they weren't willing to do the same?

Boal reflected on this experience and understood that oppression cannot be overturned when those facing the oppression aren't telling the story themselves. Any actions had to be designed collectively, through solidarity and dialogue. This led Boal to develop a series of theatre practices aimed at shifting political and social power called Theatre of the Oppressed.

WHEN TO FORUM THEATRE

What's the difference between Forum Theatre and Forum Plays?

A Forum Play is a part of Forum Theatre. A Forum Play turns into Forum Theatre when the Joker facilitates the intervention and the audience becomes a part of the scene. Forum Play + Intervention = Forum Theatre

You might turn to Forum Theatre when...

* You or your community are facing a situation of oppression. You've tried everything you can think of, and are ready to take this struggle public.
* You suspect you aren't the only person in your community facing this kind of problem.
* Traditional community organizing or advocacy tactics feel like they're not enough.
* You're looking to inject some joy or humor into otherwise serious and painful challenges.
* You are part of a creative community and want to address injustice, but you don't know how.
* You want to address an issue in a way that's more participatory and engaging, instead of another town hall, meeting, slideshow presentation, etc.

Still, there are many ways people can educate their community about an oppressive situation. People often use the news, social media, or academic approaches with numbers and data.

So why Forum Theatre?

* It reveals the human experience of a problem by tapping into the audience's feelings, and not just their logic.
* It connects those facing the problem with each other as well as with other activists and engaged community members.
* It leans into the power and expertise of those who are directly impacted.
* It empowers communities by focusing on creative alternatives and concrete actions that can be taken in the face of real problems.
* It provides the physical experience and "muscle memory" of taking action in daily life.

THE STORIES FORUM THEATRE TELLS

In its simplest form, Forum Theatre is meant to tell stories about people trying to access something they need and have a right to, but are denied.

Here's an example:

Jean-Pierre is trying to secure housing that's safe for him and his partner.

But when Jean-Pierre's landlady realizes the person moving in with him is his same-sex partner, she refuses to offer him a lease renewal.

Stress and heated arguments about what feels safe and affordable for them both eventually lead to their break up.

Instead of a Disney-like happy ending of triumph over the odds, Forum Plays end in failure so that the audience can see the problem: oppression happens when the people are denied their rights because of who they are or how they are perceived by people in power.

A good story for the Forum is:

* **Personal yet prevalent.** The story doesn't just represent one person in the acting troupe but is a problem that the whole ensemble can relate to in some way.
* **Urgent and relevant.** This issue in the story is still happening to people in the present moment, so we want to take action on it today!
* **Energizing without re-traumatizing.** While the problem should make the audience angry enough to do something, the actors developing the play hopefully have processed the oppression at least well enough to be able to talk about it publicly for the next few weeks.

Even when a story seems like a good fit, sometimes people change their minds about performing it. This isn't surprising, given how personal this work can get. In the next section, we'll explore the ethics of Forum Theatre.

THE ETHICS OF FORUM THEATRE

Some frequently asked questions about when it's ok to do Forum Theatre

"DOES THIS GROUP WANT TO DO FORUM THEATRE?"

This is a great question to ask the group directly. If they aren't familiar with Forum Theatre or T.O., show an example! (You can invite them to a performance, show a video, or even do a short demonstration of an activity.) Ask them, "What problem do you want to see change? Would you feel comfortable making a scene about it? Does this process feel right for us?"

"IS IT OK TO DO A FORUM ABOUT THIS TOPIC?"

If you have a group of people who have experienced the problem and generally agree it's happening because of systems of oppression, AND they want to talk to an audience about it, then yes, it's probably okay. If you're asking because you're worried if using Forum Theatre will be unsafe or oppressive, talk about this with the group and with people you trust to analyze the power dynamics. If you do the project, reflect on how it went, and how you would shape it next time to make it more ethical.

"IS IT ETHICAL TO ASK THIS GROUP OF PEOPLE TO SHARE THEIR STORIES?"

If you're asking because of a concern about a power dynamic in your project, it's important to think through how to communicate the intention of the project, and how much agency to give everyone to opt in or opt out when it's time to share stories. Does the group understand why they're sharing stories?

Do they know how their story will be shared and who else will hear it? Are they given the option to opt out of sharing? Has everyone fully come on board with the activist intentions of the project?

"WILL IT BE TRAUMATIC FOR THE GROUP TO ACT OUT THEIR STORIES?"

Possibly. The process of making a Forum performance means discussing, examining, and re-enacting oppressive experiences. It's important to keep this in mind as we select stories and build ways to support each other in rehearsals and performances. Forum Theatre is a tool for us to decide how to tell and change our stories. Ultimately, the Forum should leave the actors and audience thinking more about the possibilities of action and less about the traumatic incidents that inspired the play.

ASK YOURSELF

Is this the right collaboration?

Do your collaborators share your power analysis and your goals of advocacy and structural change? How do you ensure that they do before you find yourself at odds during the process? How might a difference in perspectives impact the process?

"Once, at a TONYC partner organization, a new staff person expressed concern that the young people would be framing their stories as examples of systemic failures. That is, she said, the young people should be taking responsibility for their own role in becoming homeless. She said that these young people had made mistakes. In her words, they saw themselves as victims, and this stood in the way of their success in life.

"This, in our opinion, stood in opposition to the politics and philosophy of Theatre of the Oppressed. Homelessness isn't an individual failure, but a symptom of structural inequity, poverty, racism. Overcoming oppression isn't a matter of individual efforts or 'successes'; it requires a collective, societal effort.

"From that conversation, TONYC took a different approach in partnering with organizations to create Forum Theatre troupes. We had to start with a shared political analysis, advocacy goal and an understanding that the plays would address structural oppression head-on." —Katy Rubin, Founding Executive Director

Notes

These pages are
yours! Feel free to
skip around, write
in the margins, rip
out pages, and add
your own ideas!

WHAT'S A JOKER ?

Before jumping into the nitty-gritty of facilitating Forum Theatre, we think it's helpful to reflect on the intentions, motivations, and lived experiences that make up our Jokering. Chapter 2 will help you think through what you bring to the table as a Joker, and how you can deepen your practice.

ALWAYS BECOMING A JOKER

A Joker is a facilitator who leads Games, activities, dialogue, and performance techniques of Theatre of the Oppressed.

The role is called *Joker* in reference to a Joker in a deck of cards, which doesn't belong to any suit. The role in T.O. isn't neutral, however. The Joker's agenda is to pursue concrete, ethical action against oppression with the actors and audience.

The work of TONYC Jokers is primarily to:
* Facilitate rehearsals to create a Forum Play
* Facilitate the final Forum Performance by moderating the interaction between Spect-Actors and actors.

TONYC Jokers occasionally facilitate workshops for people who want to be trained in Theatre of the Oppressed techniques.

People become Jokers through training and practice. But the training and practice continue even after someone "is" a Joker. There is no central, global authority that decides who is a Theatre of the Oppressed Joker.

You don't have to do it alone
Working with another Joker (as a team or pair of co-Jokers) is a helpful tool that can support the collaboration with actors. Facilitation takes a lot of energy and attention, and we don't expect one person to support and meet all the needs of a group. Working with a partner can help Jokers:
* Stay accountable to the troupe and the shared goals.
* Understand the varied needs of the group.
* Maintain their personal mental health.

What hats do you wear?
You probably wear many hats in your everyday life. This list of skills may help you think about what other hats might be helpful to wear while Jokering. These

Amorarey Sandoz, on how he learned to become a Joker with TONYC

"After experiencing Forum Theatre as a TONYC actor, I started training to become a Joker. The training program had a structure where it was okay to take my time and make mistakes. Learning to Joker with TONYC was like learning to operate a car in an open parking lot. I got a chance to observe experienced Jokers drive rehearsals and asked questions about how they shifted gears or made difficult maneuvers. Then when it was time for me to start running parts of rehearsal, I felt as though I was guided by cones that made the road. I still have a lot that I want to learn, and I expect some bumps in the road, but training has prepared me to take my Joker skills for a test drive into the sunset."

skills can inform your facilitation and help identify any areas where you might want additional support.

Skills you may already have, or may need to develop:

NAVIGATING INSTITUTIONS AND SYSTEMS OF OPPRESSION

Your own life experiences with systems of oppression should inform your Jokering. We say this here in case you've ever been told to leave those experiences "at the door," or not to talk about yourself if you're directing others.

STAGE MANAGEMENT OR THEATRE PRODUCTION

If you've ever managed all the details that happen offstage, you can use those skills to make plans to care for the project, the actors, and the shows. If you don't have these skills, see the section "What a Project Needs," for a checklist that can start you off (see p. 153 in the Index of Tools).

THEATRE DIRECTOR

If your project includes people who have little or no experience performing on stage, someone with experience directing plays will be able to support the actors in adapting their creative ideas into blocking and editing their scene ideas.

COMMUNITY ORGANIZER

Theatre of the Oppressed needs people in a room. So if you've spent time working to get people to show up, these skills will help bring actors into rehearsal and audiences into the room! You probably also have skills in teaching, decision-making, and meeting people where they are.

SOCIAL WORKER

You've been trained to support others. How can that inform how you design gatherings and support systems?

HEALER

Oppression traumatizes individuals and communities. As people share their stories, and engage with the systems that have impacted their lives, what support can healing bring to the process?

What's a Joker?

MISTAKES WE TRY NOT TO MAKE

Here's a list of some unhelpful mindsets we've seen when facilitating T.O. We challenge all jokers (including ourselves) to resist intentions that might undermine the ethics of the work.

I WILL TEACH PEOPLE ABOUT OPPRESSION.

If Jokers enter rehearsals, workshops, or performances thinking they will teach people about oppression, they are centering themselves as the experts. It's our expectation that every person in the room is an expert and will learn from and inform the others. This idea is central in Paulo Freire's *Pedagogy of the Oppressed*, and we invite you to read it for a deeper understanding of the perspective.

I AM UN-BIASED.

Stop! We are all biased! Because we're all embedded in systems of oppression, our biases are probably programmed to be oppressive even with the best of intentions. We need to recognize this in order to liberate ourselves.

I NEVER OPPRESS ANYONE.

How have you decided that you aren't oppressive? When we are Jokering, we ask people to do things, make decisions, and moderate discussions about oppression. It's possible we will do something that has an oppressive impact. How can we be ready to see that, and prepare ourselves to address it?

I AM SAVING OPPRESSED PEOPLE.

When we facilitate, we are building our collective awareness of how oppression works so that we all find actions and collaborations to liberate ourselves. Why do you use the word "save"? Is your own liberation complete?

I AM SERVING OPPRESSED PEOPLE.

If, as a Joker, you see yourself as an outsider, and don't expect to be impacted or find liberation in the work, ask yourself: why?

Notes

These pages are yours! Feel free to skip around, write in the margins, rip out pages, and add your own ideas!

To explore these ideas further, check out the worksheet "How Do I Relate to Power, Oppression, and Privilege?" on p. 158 in the Index of Tools.

THE TECHNIQUES WE USE

Chapter 3 covers the strategies
and techniques we use at TONYC
to make Forum Theatre with a
group of actors.

THEATRE GAMES

If you're already a theatre-maker, you might be used to playing games to warm up before a rehearsal or performance. Any exercise to activate an actor's body, voice, or ability to collaborate will strengthen the creative process. In T.O., we define an actor as anyone ready to take action in real life. We see the actor as an activist. For this reason, Jokers should prioritize T.O. Games, a technique to encourage a special kind of warm-up known as de-mechanization or good confusion.

De-mechanization is the practice of unlearning existing social structures and norms that may be harmful to ourselves and our communities. These may be more explicit concepts like "We call the police because violence has to be punished" or more subtle and implicit like "Women need to smile." Regardless, these norms and structures have been "mechanized" or programmed into our society much like a computer learning an automation.

Boal compared Theatre of the Oppressed to a tree with many branches. The technique of Forum Theatre is just one branch of Theatre of the Oppressed. To see an illustration of this tree and a description of all the techniques in T.O., jump to our Index of Tools, p. 146.

Through active and participatory Games and exercises, Jokers support actors in exploring and challenging their relationship to oppressive norms in a way that's fun and accessible. The Games are playful social metaphors that simulate, replicate, or abstract experiences that also occur in real life. During or after each Game, the Joker also leads a debrief or dialogue. These debrief conversations aim to highlight how we contend with big ideas like identity, power relations, and solidarity.

Instead of explaining these big ideas all at once, like in a diversity training, we hope these Games allow Jokers and actors to define these concepts for themselves. Establishing a shared understanding of oppressive systems and norms eventually helps a group of actors to identify the issues they want to address in their Forum Play. It also prepares the group to interact with an audience in new ways, which feels a bit like a Game itself. From warming up the audience before the show, to improvising solutions onstage during the Forum Play, every element of the performance involves active participation and flips the traditional power dynamic of "actor" vs. "audience" on its head. Using Games early in the process helps actors get into this mindset early on. *(You can find more de-mechanization Games and facilitation instructions in the Index of Tools, p. 171)*

Turn to the next page for an example of a de-mechanization Game.

NAME GUMBO
**For introducing the concept of "confusion"—
or de-mechanization—as well as names**

GROUP DEMONSTRATION

Two volunteers face each other and introduce themselves to each other. Freeze in handshake. Via handshake, names switch. Use a third volunteer to demonstrate that players continue to switch names with whoever they meet, using the last name they heard as their own.

EVERYONE PLAYS

Encourage the group to have fun and try to meet as many people as possible.

ADD NEW INSTRUCTION

"Everyone FREEZE! Do you know the name you have right now? Continue from this point, but if your own name comes back to you, step to the side and watch. Make sure you give away the name you had before you leave."

ALTERNATIVE INSTRUCTION

Let everyone reset back to having their own names.

CONTINUE PLAYING

When most are "out" and the rest are frustrated, pause game. Ask what names are still in.

DEBRIEF

* "How was that?"
  (looking for: fun, confusing, weird, hard)

* "How did it feel to introduce yourself as someone else?"

* "How did it feel to get your name back?"

* "How did it feel not to find your name?"

* "Challenges, what did people notice?"

* Introduce the "rule" of confusion: "If we aren't prepared to be a bit confused, unsure, etc., then we aren't prepared for change. We are rehearsing for the uncertainty of change."

You and your troupe might not want to do all of the exercises we listed in our Index of Tools. However, Jokers that don't bring in any play or games throughout rehearsal risk creating Forum Theatre that's fixated more on the end-product than the process. From our experiences, we've learned that not having enough games in the rehearsal process can end up feeling stale and mechanized for the actors.

If you're not feeling some of the suggested games, you can make your own! Creating new games and activities can help keep this work fresh as you continue to Joker in different spaces. On p. 160, you'll find a worksheet on how to build your own de-mechanization game.

HOW TO DEBRIEF GAMES FOR T.O.

Theatre of the Oppressed practices rely on shared experiences of activities and group discussions.

The activities (Games, scenes, performances) give us a representation of our lived experience, and the discussion allows us to reflect on and analyze the experience, especially with an eye to power dynamics and how we want to change them. Here's a short map that Jokers can apply to design their own debrief prompts:

Part 1: The Joker asks the participants questions to reflect on the experience of the activity

* First, what's a short, easy-to-answer question that'll get people talking about their experience in the activity? The intention of easy-to-answer questions is to set a level of comfort with entering the discussion. This can warm people up to the rest of the discussion. Tip: Ask a question that feels slightly obvious. "Did we get moving?" "Was that easy or hard?"

* Ask follow-up questions to make space for people to describe their experiences. "Was there a moment that was particularly hard?"

* Ask questions that invite a variety of experiences, so that other people are also heard. "Is there anyone who had a different experience?"

* Ask questions that allow people to share experiences related to the intention of the activity. Examples: "When did you notice this felt _____?" "How did power show up for you?"

Part 2. The Joker ask questions to connect the experience in the activity to life experiences

Ask questions that prompt people to connect the key experience of the Game to dynamics they experience in the real world.

Tip: Use the words people shared as part of your question. Example: "Several people said this activity made them rely on other people a lot, in ways that were uncomfortable for some, and comfortable for others. Do those feelings show up when you have to rely on people in real life?"

Part 3: The Joker wraps up the conversation

* Name the key reflections from the conversation. Or, ask the group to name them.

* Highlight particular ideas that you want the group to bring to a future activity. This could be the next activity, or an activity at a future rehearsal.

To explore these ideas further, turn to "Make Your Own T.O. Game" on p. 160 in the Index of Tools.

Omari Soulfinger on how we turned Rock Paper Scissors into an online de-mechanization Game

"The problem with 'Rock Paper Scissors' on Zoom is that it's more complicated to pair off, so in the online adaptation you're in grid view but don't know who you're actually competing against! The modification is: Just choose someone but don't tell them they are your opponent. This was practical at first but then became a metaphor. The feelings of paranoia, being watched while also watching and trying to dominate...you don't know if your opponents are cheating or if you might get away with cheating! In the debrief, the Joker could ask, "How does this thinking and this response to competition show up in systems of oppression?" I remember once someone introduced a new gesture (not a rock, scissor, or paper gesture) into the Game...and then boom, the whole activity and metaphor were disrupted... fantastic. 'Rock' 'Paper' and 'Scissors' are just choices given by the power figure—in this case, the Joker—so how wonderful when someone uses their own divine creativity to make a choice on how to interact."

IMAGE THEATRE

The next key technique for building Forum Theatre is called Image Theatre. While de-mechanization Games lead Jokers and actors to use metaphors and discussions to reveal truths about our world, Image Theatre helps move the group to embody those truths and share visual stories to represent them.

In Image Theatre exercises, actors create a frozen or still image with their bodies, in response to a prompt offered by the Joker. Image Theatre always begins with a physical gesture or shape, without words.

Image Theatre exercises can look like:

* Jokers asking actors to use their bodies to create a sculpture-image of the word "happy." In the next round, Jokers ask actors to use their bodies to create a sculpture-image for the term "prison system."
* Jokers asking two volunteers shake hands and then saying, "Freeze!" Jokers then ask the other participants to describe what they see.

The joy of Image Theatre lies in the power of nonverbal communication. If your group has gotten into some heated debates after the Game debriefs, Image Theatre may be a way for the actors to start to find connection and commonality again. And as a Joker facilitates these exercises, the group begins performing, without feeling the pressure of "acting."

The nonverbal magic of these techniques also comes in handy when a Joker wants to introduce how power can impact the relationship between two or more people. Actors typically find it easy (and fun) to come up with ways to show power relations or dynamics. Activities like **Image of the Word** (on p. 189 and the next page) and **Complete the Image** (on p. 191) help build confidence in sharing stories and build the muscle of analyzing power in scenes.

Letitia Bouie
(former actor, TONYC Joker)

"The most fun I've had playing with the Concrete Justice troupe happened when we learned something new. Like with Image Theatre exercises, images bring emotions to life..."

IMAGE OF THE WORD (Image Theatre)

GROUP DEMONSTRATION

Make a big circle, facing out. When the Joker gives a word or phrase, build your body into a sculpture/image of that word, using facial expressions as well as your full range of movement. After everyone has had a chance to build their sculpture, count "1, 2, 3, Image" and everyone turns around to face in and see all the images.

EVERYONE PLAYS

Start with warm-up words that are lighter in theme: birthday, beach, or maybe the city you're in (e.g., New York). Move on to use words fthat have come up in rehearsal so far: education, health care, social worker, etc. While each person holds their image, everyone is invited to say aloud the things they see around the circle. That can be feelings, or movements, or ideas: "Anger." "Bored." "Arms closed, protective." "Mean teacher." Anything they see and say is great.

ADD A NEW INSTRUCTION

While holding their image, participants can move into "families"—other images that fit with theirs. All the groups can look at the other families one by one and talk about what they see. That family can all add a sound: something they can repeat that evokes their image. Add: everyone in that group can speak a word, or make a repetitive movement, that their image wants to make. Add: dubbing (step in and say what that character is saying/thinking). These families can turn into story-sharing groups on a specific topic pretty seamlessly.

DEBRIEF

* *"Did anything surprise you about any of these words / topics?"*
* *"If you used the 'families' to move into groups for sharing stories of oppression towards creating a play—how was that process? Did you discover any alignment?"*

In Image Theatre activities, the Joker should ask the troupe to reflect on what the details of each image communicates to the audience with questions like:

* *"What does it mean that Roland is leaning forward and Andrew is leaning away?"*

* *"How is this image different now that Solange has a closed fist instead of an open fist?"*

* *"Someone said this looks like a mother and a daughter. What does it say about their relationship now that the mother is reaching out with her palms down instead of up?"*

An important part of any Forum Theatre performance is to show how individuals, groups of people, and institutions wield power.

Performances benefit from actors who know how to convey power on stage, even through subtle gestures. Image Theatre exercises help actors learn how to use their bodies, voices, and movements to convey power dynamics without much dialogue. Beyond the Forum, doing this also helps the activist mind to be able to name what oppression looks like out in the real world.

"I think Bill might have more power than Shaniece because he's taking up more space on the bench with his legs."

Jokers may find it useful to use Image Theatre techniques even after the group has a story they are trying to stage. Jokers can regularly ask questions about gestures and relationships between bodies to build everyone's awareness of the story being told by images. They can use prompts like the ones below to help actors stage their story:

* **Beginning.** "*Make an image of how you felt when you found a therapist you liked.*"
* **Middle.** "*Make an image of how it felt fighting with the insurance company.*"
* **End.** "*Make an image of how it felt when you realized you couldn't afford therapy anymore.*"

These techniques take practice. It isn't always easy to get a group to explore images without words. Most people's instinct is to explain their idea first. We've found that in American culture particularly, physical expression can feel uncomfortable or strange. Taking race and ethnicity into account: asking someone to "freeze" or "stop moving" might trigger unexpected emotions. Jokers can develop skills to ease actors into the process, but it takes time, patience and playing with different activities. (Many of these activities even have steps for the Joker to add sound and movement to the image, which can relieve the silence!)

AESTHETICS OF THE OPPRESSED

As you've probably come to see, Theatre of the Oppressed isn't just about theatre. The next technique–Aesthetics of the Oppressed–is a way of using art forms other than theatre to express ourselves and share what we experience.

Jokers can use the <mark>Aesthetics of the Oppressed</mark> to support actors in creating poems, paintings, sculptures, music, and even comedy gags. Aesthetics activities aren't about teaching the actors how to sing or paint in a particular style. Instead, these activities make space for us to develop and express the creativity, beauty, and musicality we already possess.

Using Aesthetics of the Oppressed to create an abstract representation of the problem in your play can serve two purposes: engaging actors in the aesthetic process and creating aesthetic products.

The Aesthetic Process is the making of the art. The art made from this technique should focus on the emotional experience of the problem, not the narrative details of the story in the play. Whenever Jokers include these techniques in rehearsal, the whole troupe has an opportunity to emotionally connect with each other and to share their emotional experiences related to the problems in the play. This act of sharing experiences and art can deepen actors' sense of solidarity with each other. There are lots of different ways to use art-making to share emotional experiences. These could include writing poems, drawing pictures, choreographing a dance, etc.

We caution any Joker who thinks this process isn't a priority. The emotional experience of a problem is critical information, and a Joker should work with actors to find ways to infuse the play with this information and communicate it to the audience. For this reason, Jokers should ask the troupe what images from these activities resonate with them.

Sulu LeoNimm,
founding member and
Executive Director

"Our most famous and popular prop is our 'White Guy Tie,' which is a giant, white tie that hangs down to most actors' knees, says 'White Guy' on the front, and clarifies the racial and gender dynamics of the character regardless of the race/gender of the actor wearing it."

The other purpose of delving into Aesthetics of the Oppressed is to create an **Aesthetic Product**—something to be shared with the audience that will enlighten them regarding the actors' perspective.

Here are some ways an Aesthetic Product might end up in your final Forum Theatre Performance.

You might create an Aesthetic Product to artistically depict any moments that are too traumatic to be staged literally.
In *Nature of the Crime,* a play about the oppression experienced within reentry programs, an actor performs a poem about the domestic violence she suffered before being incarcerated for an act of self-defense.

You can also use any imagery or figurative language (metaphors, personification, hyperbole, puns) that come up in the Aesthetics exercises in the final performance.
When creating *Masc Off,* our actors described how performing masculinity while depressed often felt like wearing a mask in public. Throughout the show, whenever characters were pretending to be fine, they held a literal mask in front of their face.

Using comedy and musical transitions between scenes is a great way to give the audience a quick breath between the stressful realities of the Forum scenes.
Connecticut Mental Health Center actors had a scene of a Protagonist showing up in front of a shelter. One actor held up a poster board that represented the shelter door, and told the Protagonist all the things that were wrong with the shelter. When the Protagonist asked what he should do instead of walking inside, the actor with the poster board replied, "Don't ask me, I'm just a door!"

on how he uses dark comedy to help
actors and audiences feel empowered
while staging oppression

Omari Soulfinger

"Exaggeration is how I blow up the contradiction and the pain until it's completely absurd. Sometimes the exaggeration could be literal, giving the Antagonist a huge novelty prop, or a really over-the-top melodramatic accent. Usually, we exaggerate how explicit and obvious the oppression is because the coded subtle and subversive ways these things happen really hit too close to home."

Both the Aesthetic Process and Aesthetic Product should facilitate folks learning via their senses what they already knew to be true about the world.

By tapping into people's emotional experiences, the Aesthetics of the Oppressed help uncover deep truths that may have been buried underneath internalized oppression.

For more detailed instructions on how to assign or facilitate "Aesthetics of the Oppressed Activities", see the Index of Tools (see p. 195).

Use the next page to reflect on all the techniques in this chapter. Check out the following worksheets in the Index of Tools:
‣ "From Aesthetic Process to Product" (p. 161)
‣ "Make your own T.O. game" (p. 160)

The Wildcard Workbook

Notes

These pages are
yours! Feel free to
skip around, write
in the margins, rip
out pages, add your
own ideas!

HOW TO PRACTICE JOKERING

If you've gotten this far, hopefully you have a sense for the techniques and tools you can use to build a Forum Play.

Chapters 4-7 talk about how to apply these tools in your practice, when you might use them in each step of the process, and a little bit about why. Starting with a birds-eye view of setting up a Forum Theatre process with a new troupe, the following chapters take a deeper dive into both playmaking and the final Forum Performance.

4. T.O. IN ACTION: A WEEK-BY-WEEK OVERVIEW
5. BUILDING THE PLAY
6. ENGAGING SPECT-ACTORS
7. BEYOND THE FORUM

T.O. IN ACTION: A WEEK-BY-WEEK OVERVIEW

Chapter 4 goes over TONYC's week-by-week process to help you plan out your rehearsals. You can adapt the Weekly Planning Template to meet your group's specific timing and needs.

TONYC, WEEK-BY-WEEK

When TONYC partners with community organizations to do Forum Theatre, we usually spend between 10 and 12 weeks building and performing a play with a new troupe.

Once a week, TONYC co-Joker pairs will meet the troupe on site to rehearse for about 2 hours at a time. After about 16 hours of rehearsal, the troupe should have something ready to present and Forum with an audience.

The following overview of TONYC's process shows how we pace ourselves to build the play and includes our best practices and some challenges that come up along the way.

We know different groups might have different time restraints. Use the planning tool on p. 149 to create a plan that fits your group's needs!

Week 0
BEFORE YOUR
FIRST REHEARSAL

Weeks 1–2
EXPLORATION

Weeks 3–5
CREATION

Weeks 6–8
REHEARSAL

Week 9
FINAL PERFORMANCE(S)

Week 10
WRAP UP

WEEK 0, BEFORE YOUR FIRST REHEARSAL

Because we've done it before, we do not recommend coming in for a first rehearsal trying to convince people that they are being oppressed. Instead, this time should be a recruitment period. This is a good time to gather a group of people who:

* Are excited to collaborate on something creative and performative.

* Have real life stories of oppression that they are willing to share.

* Believe in the power of collective action and community organizing.

That said, even if you are working with a partner organization that has done a great job of registering participants for your "theatre program," you shouldn't assume that there is 100% buy-in or understanding of the process.

Liz Morgan,
Director of Training
& Pedagogy, TONYC

"At the first rehearsal, I usually tell a personal story about why I love this work or get an alumni actor to help spread the word about why they think Forum Theatre is meaningful. But I also think it's okay to accept that folks may not fully appreciate this work until they've seen it through to the end, and Jokers can encourage folks to stay curious and trust the process."

WEEKS 1-2
EXPLORATION

The goal of our early rehearsals is to explore and connect.

Jokers can put together a combination of Games and activities to introduce Theatre of the Oppressed, and offer actors the opportunity to learn about each other. Through de-mechanization Games and debriefing conversations, the Joker and actors start talking about the social norms and structures that impact them. This builds the foundation for the play-building process.

After playing several Games, you may introduce the concept of Forum Theatre to your troupe of actors. There are a few different ways to do this, including showing a full Forum Theatre play or recording if you have those resources available. We typically use the following activities:

* Performing a Forum Demo, to show actors how Forum Theatre works.
* Drawing a Story Arc, to show actors the structure of a Forum Play.

Setting up a Forum Demo exercise
A Forum Demo is simply a demonstration of how Forum Theatre works. Actors will jump into an improvisation about an abstract metaphor for a human right.

For example, in the **Handshake Forum Demo,** the Protagonist is denied their right to receive a handshake, and the troupe gets to try their first Intervention.

This Forum Demo Exercise is a great way to have folks interact with the structure of a Forum and it will help for them to know how Forum Theatre works even if the actors haven't decided on a theme for their Forum Play. As you debrief the Handshake Forum Demo, you can start to ask your actors what the handshake could represent.

In the Handshake Forum the right to a "handshake" often inspires folks to explore literal and tangible needs like food or housing. The Marcher's Forum uses the right to "dance," which is great for prompting folks to discuss more intangible human needs like the right to express one's sexuality. (Go to p. 185 for instructions on facilitating and debriefing the Handshake Forum Demo and the Marchers Forum Demo.)

WEEKS 1-2 EXPLORATION

How to structure a Forum Play

This story arc helps show the key parts of a Forum Play:

* A Protagonist with a need (specifically a human right).
* An Antagonist that denies their right to access this need.
* The injustice when the Protagonist fails to get their needs met (or the system fails them!).

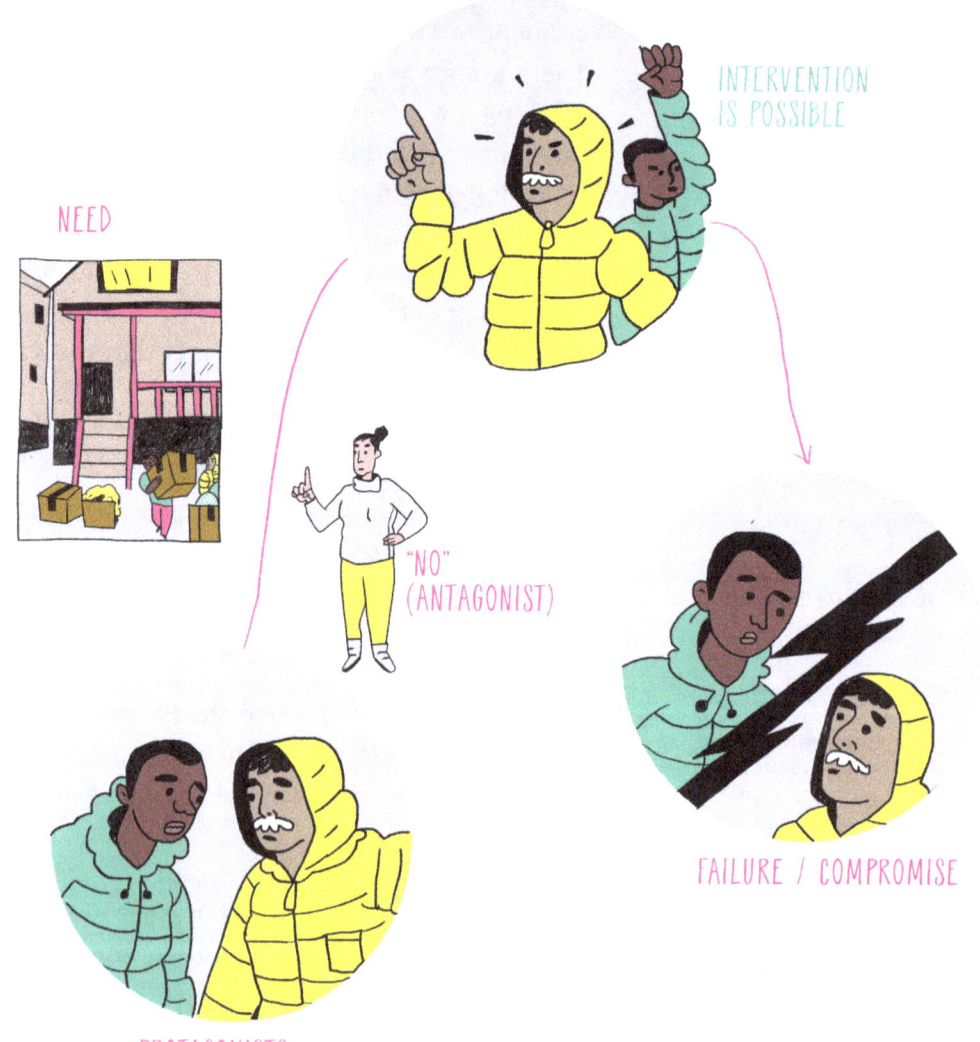

NEED

INTERVENTION IS POSSIBLE

"NO" (ANTAGONIST)

FAILURE / COMPROMISE

PROTAGONISTS

For more on details on this structure, jump to p. 75 where we'll go into using this story arc in more detail.

Mike Gonzalez,
former actor and TONYC Joker

"For me, one of the hardest parts of the rehearsal process is having to navigate the discussions and debriefs after introducing folks to what T.O. is about. Oftentimes the conversations get deep, personal, or thought-provoking, and it's difficult not to delve into them for the duration of rehearsal! Obviously, because of time restraints and the structure of creating the play, a Joker has to guide the conversation toward keeping the rehearsal flowing."

When debriefing any Forum Demo Exercise, Jokers should make sure to remind the troupe that the activity is just a demo, and no decisions have been made yet about the play. This is a good moment to invite the troupe to reflect on the structure of the play and the issues they'd like to investigate.

We've discovered that these early sessions are a good time to explore what it means to be in community and solidarity as a troupe. You can start this conversation by setting up Group Agreements on your first or second session. Many of our Jokers also use these rehearsals to figure out what sorts of rituals help the troupe to feel valued. Holding time at the beginning and end of gatherings to meditate, check in, and close out are some of TONYC's favorite go-tos.

We also use non-theatre activities and exercises to build a shared vocabulary around systemic oppression. For example, the **(Anti)Oppression Lens** (explained in detail in our Index of Tools on p. 168) can be used to get actors thinking about ways to depict different kinds of oppression.

For tips on how to facilitate Group Agreements and other group discussions, go to Group Discussion Tools on p. 165 in the Index of Tools.

WEEKS 3-5 CREATION

After a few weeks of exploration, we encourage our Jokers to start creating something with the troupe! But this isn't to say that exploration or de-mechanization ever stops! It's great to bring in new Games or even return to old ones to warm up your actors for each part of the Forum Theatre-making process. But in these weeks, Jokers should get actors to explicitly collaborate on making theatre and art based on social justice issues that impact their communities.

If you haven't been given a prompt by the community organization you are partnered with, pay close attention to the early debriefs and conversations. Topics and themes tend to come up organically. In any case, Jokers will likely need to come up with a strategy for getting the actors to start telling personal stories. And if you don't have a story-sharing strategy, don't worry! We got you on p. 78-90.

During the creation process, Image Theatre and Aesthetics exercises can be useful tools to move the troupe towards a full Forum Play. You can also use these techniques before the narrative of your play has been defined to get folks comfortable with each other, and with sharing their personal stories.

GROUP DECISION-MAKING

As you hone in on themes, stories, narrative details, etc., more and more decisions will need to be made about the content of the Forum Play. TONYC Jokers are encouraged to support the troupe in making most artistic decisions as a collective (as opposed to Jokers imposing their ideas onto the troupe). There are many ways to do this work. A Joker may look for consensus, present a proposal and ask if everyone is in agreement, or vote. This workbook won't be able to give you a one-size-fits-all approach to group decision-making. But with this icon ✳, we'll identify moments when Jokers use tools and strategies for group decision-making.

Once the troupe has a rough outline of the narrative that they are ready to collaborate on, they may hesitate to "get up on their feet" and embody the story. Sometimes actors have a strong sense of what the characters should say but have trouble envisioning how to show it on stage. Other times, actors may feel intimidated by the idea of improvising the dialogue.

Image Theatre can be used to support both scenarios. A facilitator can help actors dynamize, or bring to life, three frozen images (beginning-middle-end) into a physically fluid **Scene-without-Words (p. 193).** In this activity, some actors in the troupe can do the pantomime while others help add dialogue by narrating what's happening. This way multiple actors can collaborate on devising the work and adding their understanding of power and oppression to the storytelling.

Another de-mechanization exercise that might support actors in staging power is **The Great Game of Power (p. 183).** Similar to **Complete the Image (p. 191)**, this warm-up will get participants thinking about how to organize set pieces, like chairs, in a way that shows a power dynamic.

WHO'S
ATTENDING
THE SHOW?

Usually between weeks 3 and 5, Jokers and actors should decide who their intended audience is. Maybe they want to build solidarity with peers who have experienced the same kind of oppression. Maybe they want to challenge people in power who enable this kind of oppression. Make sure you, the Joker, have this conversation with your troupe and make time inside and outside of rehearsal to curate a list of individuals, communities, or organizations who should be invited. At TONYC, Jokers do this in collaboration with the administrative staff because this is a lot of work!

WEEKS 6-8 REHEARSAL

Letitia Bouie,
former actor and current
TONYC Joker

"My favorite rehearsal game is **Genres.** When you facilitate it, actors first play out their roles as they would in a normal rehearsal. As time goes by, someone yells out a genre like "Soap Opera" and then actors get to play out the same scene in that style. Western, Comedy, Action, Martial Arts, Kids Show and Horror are other examples you can use. The characters may become funnier or change the dynamic of the scene. As an actor, Genres gives me the space to try whatever is given to me."

People often ask, "Who writes your plays?" And we usually say, "No one!" A Forum Play does NOT need to be scripted.

The play's dialogue should primarily happen through the improvisation of the actors. At TONYC, we find the process of memorizing lines often distracts our actors from being present during the unscripted Interventions. So most, if not all of our Forum Plays are performed as structured improvisation. That said, if the actors think it would be helpful sometimes to have a part scripted or a one-pager with key moments outlined, Jokers can write it up for the troupe.

In the weeks leading up to the performance, you should have an actual play to rehearse and fine-tune. By fine-tuning, we mean filling in those details that make the characters feel three-dimensional and make the situations seem real. For example a rough draft of a play may have a character called "broke baby daddy," but in a fine-tuned draft, the actor would know the character's name (Gordon), his specific relationship to the Protagonist (on and off for 10 years), and how he survives (picking up cans and bottles to exchange for money). However, filling in these fine details is still different than drafting a full script of the play, with all the dialogue written down.

Rehearsal Games like **Opera, Genre(s), Interior Monologue, or Interrogation** (see the Index of Tools) will help actors explore and know their characters and their circumstances more deeply. (Even the oppressor has feelings and those feelings are what motivate him to change—or not change—during the Interventions!)

DETAILS MATTER

Make sure that small details like a character's age or the location of a scene contribute to the overall goals of the Forum. For example, in one play called *2 angry 2 talk,* a set of twins gets bullied at school about not having a mom and later try to ask their father about seeing a therapist to cope with the grief of their mother's death. Making the characters twins was a choice that felt fun but also made it easy to build a scene in which the Protagonists could be in the same classroom at school. In an earlier draft, an actor played the father's girlfriend as a "gold-digging" evil stepmother-to-be, which was a fun role to act. But this choice didn't help the play focus on mental health stigmas because it was too easy for the dialogue to focus on whether Dad should dump the evil girlfriend. We eventually changed this character to be more empathetic: an ally who agreed with the twins but didn't have the power to advocate for them because she wasn't a legal guardian. Have a group check-in and ask the troupe: What will help the audience see the problem? How can we make our story more clear?

As the group makes final decisions to fine-tune character details, think through how these details will play out in the Forum performance.

Eventually, you'll have to have discussions about casting. This can be very tricky because actors might have a lot of feelings about this. Actors who have built up a decent amount of solidarity will hopefully be focused on presenting the problem clearly instead of stealing the spotlight from one another. If you're working on a story very heavily based on the experiences of one particular individual, encourage this person to play anyone BUT the Protagonist. Aside from making the process feel more balanced and collaborative, this person will probably understand the Antagonist very intimately and be best suited for that role. This will also help avoid some of the trauma that surrounds re-enacting their own

WEEKS 6-8 REHEARSAL

story. The **Boxing Activity** on p. 198 in the Index of Tools is also a good way to "audition" which actors feel comfortable holding the core argument of the Forum play which will prepare them for the Forum Interventions. ✳

FLEXIBLE CASTING

It's not uncommon for troupes to feel extra stressed right before the show. This is especially true when people are late or absent, which often happens because of the same forces of oppression that the plays are about (e.g., appointments, police harassment, stressful jobs). For this reason we try to prepare everyone to be ready to step in for any role!

In the earlier creation weeks, you may have used Aesthetics of the Oppressed to imagine Aesthetic Products as costumes or props. (For more, see p. 195) Make sure these elements have actually been created and rehearsed.

In general, we think it's important to the ethics of Theatre of the Oppressed to have actors decide on, design, and make the technical elements that help tell the story on stage.

Sometimes these elements are very practical and small—like the receptionist's phone at the doctor's office, or a painted bus-stop sign, for example. These elements are also an opportunity for actors to add their own style to the play in a new way, especially when the creation of those elements is rooted in Aesthetics of the Oppressed. The design elements then support us in asking the question that Forum Play is meant to ask. Especially if there are actors in your troupe who have shied away from the scene work, you might engage them in creating poetry, song, costumes, props, backdrops, show art, etc. ✳

By this point, actors should feel comfortable with all the technical and design elements and know where everything goes. Jokers can support the troupe by making a simple, easy-to-read outline of the show, with notes about technical details, such as which sounds, lights, and key dialogue moments are cues.

It's also important that actors know what to wear and who is responsible for providing costume items. Any decision made too last-minute could really throw off actors and affect their performance, so try to rehearse with as many elements as possible during your final dress rehearsal. (For more, see p. 94 on Preparing Your Actors.)

WEEK 9
FINAL
PERFORMANCE

The week leading up to the performance is still about supporting your troupe. This is pretty different from the high stress "HELL week" some theatre practitioners might be used to.

The goal of this whole process is to resist harmful power dynamics, and this holds true for performance day too. So resist the urge to let the stress you're feeling transform into a domineering attitude towards the group.

It's helpful to meet your actors at the performance venue at least 30 minutes before the event starts. If the day of the performance is the first time your actors will see this space, we recommend meeting them even earlier, so they have time to get familiar with the space.

This "call" time largely depends on how many technical elements your show has. If there are lights, make sure your actors can be seen. Maybe there are sound cues or microphones. Make sure your actors can be heard, too. Actors appreciate having time to get familiar with the space and will want to know where are safe spaces to store valuables, change clothes, eat dinner, or use the bathroom. Jokers and actors should also make any necessary decisions about how/where entrances and exits happen on stage. If there isn't time to run through the entire play, the actors should at the very least warm up their group improvisation skills together, ideally on stage and before the house is opened up to your public audience.

Jump to the **Performance Day Checklist** in the Index of Tools (p. 156) that we've made for your convenience. Before you know it, it will be time for the audience to see all your hard work. "Break a leg", as they say!

Our **TONYC "Joker Script Flash Cards"** in Chapter 6 (p. 93) include facilitation notes for a welcome, warm-up Games, performing and watching the play, Interventions, and a debrief.

DE-MECHANIZE YOUR JOKERING

By *script* we don't mean something that must be memorized. Just like our Forum plays, the *Joker Script* is structured improvisation. There are important points to hit, but as you gain more skills you can and should deviate from anything that seems rote. #AlwaysDe-mechanize

WEEK 10
WRAP- UP

After you've closed your Forum Play performances, the troupe deserves to celebrate! This doesn't need to be on the same day, but it does require some facilitation (party hosting, if you will) to be intentional. Many TONYC troupes take a pause to regroup between the close of one show and the start of a new project.

We see our work with troupes as long term. The goal is to expand notions of community beyond each rehearsal process and continue to build plays together for as long as our funding and partnerships will allow. Here are some components that a final "Wrap Party" might include:

REVOLUTIONARY REST

Wait, why stop there? Can't we keep going? Of course! Feel free to design your meetings any way you like, especially if you have funds and capacity. You might even keep touring the same show for years and years. But it's useful to build in breaks of 1-4 weeks. Being intentional about setting time for breaks will help you and the actors take the time to reflect, recharge, and recommit to the Forum. Prioritizing rest is an important part of the process, and, in many ways, is radical!

Celebration

The intention here is to honor what people created and achieved, and to allow the group to name what feels worth celebrating to them. ✳

For many groups this might even mean prayer, which even a non-religious Joker can make space for. Along with food, music, or dancing, consider if there's a new activity you want to share or a troupe favorite Game that an actor wants to initiate. One of our go-to celebration activities is called "Paper Plate Awards." Sort of like a yearbook superlative, an award ribbon made out of a paper plate is given to each actor, recognizing something special they brought to the work (for example: Best Singer, Most Patient, Funniest Puns).

Reflection

The intention here, much like the actual Forum, is to open up a conversation about how the Forum Performance felt and what it did. Ask your actors how this process went for them. You can also facilitate a group conversation about the positives and negatives of their experiences (often called "Glows and Grows"). At TONYC, we sometimes ask actors to fill out a survey, which helps us to document troupe feedback over the years. We build time into our process for getting feedback so we won't miss the opportunity to become better Jokers. Especially if the performance didn't go as expected, this is an important moment to debrief and maybe even decompress from anything that may have caused harm or trauma in the last days of the process.

Action

The intention here, again much like the Forum, is to imagine what the next steps might be (what could week 11 look like? Week 15??). The Joker's goal is to pursue concrete and ethical actions, so let your actors discuss and decide what's next. ✳

Was there a new advocacy initiative mentioned at the Forum that you all will commit to as a troupe? When will rehearsals for the next Forum start? Is there an upcoming Joker training someone might want to attend? How can the troupe stay in touch with you, the Joker, or other arts and activist organizations? Many actors come to TONYC through programming at our partner organizations. This is an important moment for us to let the troupe know we aren't abandoning them just because the Forum is over. They're now part of a community that's much larger than the troupe!

**STAYING
ON TRACK**

You probably know this, but as you plan your agenda week-to-week, things will not go exactly as planned. An activity may run overtime. You may get interrupted or need to pause for an emergency. Here are some questions to ask yourself to get back on track before showtime:

* How important is the activity that was missed? Did you still get to the objective of the day with other Games?

* Is there room to ask your actors to reflect on something at home between rehearsals? Would it be ethical to assign a bit of homework? (Does the troupe have capacity for this?)

* Is there a short or simplified version of the activity that you can do?

* Can you get to the same activity next week?

* Can you pivot the debrief of the Game so that it addresses a group dynamic that has become problematic?

* What would it mean to redesign the final performance? Does the Forum need to be public?

* Is there another T.O. technique we can use besides Forum Theatre that would also lead this group to direct action?

Check out the Weekly Planning Template on p. 149 in the Index of Tools!

Notes

These pages are
yours! Feel free to
skip around, write
in the margins, and
rip out pages, add
your own ideas!

BUILDING THE PLAY

Chapter 5 covers techniques that Jokers use to successfully build a Forum Play with a group of actors.

WHAT MAKES A FORUM PLAY?

The most basic Forum Play needs at least one Protagonist. The Protagonist doesn't have something they need to survive and thrive. But it's their right to have this need met, just like anyone else.

In our earlier example, Jean-Pierre is the Protagonist who needs safe housing for himself and his partner.

At the climax of the scene, we will see the Protagonist trying to get something they need and have a right to but encountering at least one Antagonist (also known as the oppressor or a gatekeeper). The Antagonist prevents the Protagonist from getting what they need. The Antagonist operates inside an oppressive system and culture that allows for human rights to be denied, based on the identity of the Protagonist. In other words, there is an oppressive ideology like racism or homophobia at work here on both an interpersonal and a structural level.

So in the Jean-Pierre example, the landlady is the Antagonist. When she realizes his same-sex partner is moving in, she refuses to offer a lease renewal.

Forum Plays reject "happy endings"
When the audience of Spect-ators first sees the play, the story ends in failure. Maybe the Protagonist doesn't get what they need at all, or maybe the play ends in an unsatisfying compromise.

In our earlier example, Jean-Pierre and his partner break up.

Here are some other ways Jean-Pierre's story could end:

Jean-Pierre and his partner end up living on the street.

OR

Jean-Pierre renews his lease and is no longer allowed visitors because he's queer.

Whatever the scenario is, the Protagonist does not see justice in the Forum Play. This lack of satisfaction moves us into the next part of the performance, where the Joker guides the audience into a re-enactment of the climactic scene. This is called the Intervention.

The climax, when the Intervention happens, should always depict a moment of crisis in which it's possible to intervene. It's important that an action can be taken at the end of the scene, or else Forum can't happen. The climax shouldn't end in a "firing-squad" moment where the Protagonist is, for example, backed against a wall with guns pointed at them. We define a firing-squad moment as a scenario in which the person being oppressed cannot do anything differently because it's too dangerous.

The Intervention happens at a critical moment in the play, when the Protagonist's need can either be denied or recognized. At this point, an audience member—now considered a Spect-Actor—replaces the Protagonist. They put themselves in the Protagonist's shoes with the goal of getting their need met. This is another reason the crisis should be one in which Intervention is possible.

Firing-squad moments risk putting the blame on the victim by implying that there was something they could have done to prevent the oppression. The Forum process isn't interested in this line of thinking. It also doesn't require that we solve the problem presented, or even that we point out all the things the Protagonist could've done differently to change the situation. Instead, Interventions expose the truth of how oppressive systems function, and help reveal ways we can navigate them in the future. Remember, the Forum is a rehearsal for real life!

So in the Jean-Pierre example, the Spect-Actor who steps in decides to meet with a lawyer. This creates a new ending. The lawyer gives Jean-Pierre some good advice about his rights but also explains how expensive and time consuming it'll be to sue the landlady.

"Firing-Squad" Moment

A more common example of a "firing-squad" moment might be a scene that depicts sexual assault or domestic violence. A Forum Play that includes that sort of scene might have a point of Intervention *after* the assault, when the survivor is seeking justice but being oppressed by the doctors or the police.

Let's take a look at what Jean-Pierre's story looks like when mapped onto the same story-arc diagram as before:

MOMENT OF CRISIS

Jean-Pierre does not see justice. He is blocked from human rights.

ANTAGONIST OR GATEKEEPER

The landlord refuses to rent to Jean-Pierre and his partner

NEED

Jean-Pierre needs to find housing for himself and his partner

PROTAGONIST

Jean-Pierre

Jean-Pierre ends up living by himself

FAILURE OR COMPROMISE

Jean-Pierre and his partner end up homeless

Jean-Pierre and his partner break up

Now let's look at what happens to the play during the Forum with the audience:

ANTAGONIST OR GATEKEEPER

INTERVENTION IS POSSIBLE

LEASE

An audience-member turned Spect-Actor replaces the actor playing Jean-Pierre and acts out an alternative. For example: Calling a lawyer

NEED

THE ENDING CHANGES (A LOT OR A LITTLE BIT)

Court fees are too expensive for the character.

PROTAGONIST

Joker facilitates discussion about what changed

At TONYC, we call the structure of a Forum Play the "Dramaturgy." Dramaturgy impacts the performance and thus the rehearsals. Understanding the structure of a Forum Play is an extremely useful tool for Jokers!

At the performance

If the dramaturgy is strong, then it has what it needs to support the Joker in asking the audience critical questions. The Joker should never have to explicitly define oppression or power for the audience. The actors show these concepts through staging and dialogue. The play itself provokes the audience to name the problem and what it looks like.

At rehearsal

A Joker knows what a play with strong dramaturgy looks like, and uses the elements in the story arc to ask the actors key questions, start conversations, and provide any context or research that would support the troupe in telling their story.

When a play isn't grounded in strong dramaturgy, the Forum runs the risk of...

* Blaming the victim or someone else who isn't in a position of power.
* Oversimplifying the problem and/or the stakes of the failure.
* Insulting the community of actors.

Actors have spent weeks being vulnerable and sharing their own stories. If their experiences are questioned and challenged publicly, this can cause a lot of harm. So one way to avoid this is by staying rooted in the dramaturgy.

A play with a clear structure and moment of crisis helps ensure the performance is focused on the point of Forum Theatre—to engage with the audience and brainstorm solutions to an obvious injustice. An unclear play means the audience is wasting time figuring out what the problem is instead of taking action to solve it.

TECHNIQUES FOR STORY-SHARING

Telling stories of our own oppression isn't easy. T.O. practitioners around the world have many different ways of finding the narrative that will become the focus of their Forum Play. A Joker should be ready for actors to struggle with telling their stories. Some may have never shared the experience with people outside their close circles. At TONYC we often find our play by using a three-part story-sharing process during weeks 3-5 of rehearsal.

Step 1: Prompt the troupe to think of a personal experience of oppression that falls into the dramaturgy structure. You may remind them of the Forum Demo to clarify how the different parts of a story fit into the structure. The prompt could look something like this: "This week, think of a time when you tried to get something you needed and were denied because of who you are or who the oppressor thought you were." It's helpful to remind the actors to come to rehearsal with a story that they feel ready to share and talk about. Let them sleep on it if there's time in your rehearsal schedule.

Step 2: Invite folks to share their stories out loud. There are many ways to approach this, but we recommend starting with letting folks share in pairs or small groups before sharing with the whole group. These stories are the raw material that the troupe brings to their Forum Theatre performance. This part can feel scary and liberating all at once, and often requires that the Joker cares not only about theatre-making, but also for the people who might be triggered or traumatized.

Step 3: Support the troupe in deciding which stories will be the focus of the play. Facilitating this step depends on the context and dynamics of the group. It could take 15 minutes or several rehearsals to get clarity on your decision. The troupe will be best prepared to make a play about a problem that most people in the room have experience in and want to change. The central question to ask when deciding is:

What problem do we want to show in our play?

* If the stories that come up reflect a range of problems, Jokers can draw up a list and lead a discussion to map out how many actors have stories relating to each issue. You can build solidarity by asking the actors if they have ever had the same need, met the same oppressor, or been treated the same way. The visualization and storytelling can highlight one or two key themes that the group wants to focus on.

* If the group was invited to gather because of a particular issue, the Jokers should guide the process to understand which experiences the actors most want to highlight.

FINDING STORIES THAT WORK

Once actors come to rehearsal with their personal stories (from their story-sharing homework in Step 1), there's a chance that some of the stories they share won't be a good fit for Forum Theatre. Use the following scenarios to help assess which stories will work best for Forum Theatre.

Scenario 1: An actor tells a story where their problem eventually gets solved…

Does it work? Maybe

WHY?

If the troupe changed the facts of the story so that it ended in failure, would it represent the experiences of many others in a similar situation? If the troupe moves away from the individual experience of that actor and towards collective storytelling, it might still work!

Scenario 2: An actor tells a story of how she was fighting for someone else's human rights…

Does it work? Maybe

WHY?

Tread carefully here. You want to create Theatre of the Oppressed not Theatre *for* the Oppressed. Maybe her story is not the arc of the Protagonist but an ally character in a scene. How will you Joker the performance in a way that clarifies whose experience the audience is here to support? Is there someone else in the troupe who has experienced the kind of oppression that this other actor witnessed? Can you build a longer play together that shows multiple parts of this system?

Scenario 3: An actor tells a story where he didn't actually fight to get what he needed...

WHY?

In Forum Theatre the Protagonist has to try to get what they need.

* If the climax of the story is a "firing-squad" moment, it's not a good moment of Intervention for the Forum because that means the Protagonist didn't fight because he couldn't fight. HOWEVER, this doesn't mean you can't include this moment in your Forum Play, but perhaps there's something that happened afterwards or before this moment that will be better for the Forum.

* If he didn't fight because he felt unsure of what to say or do, this uncertainty might be better unpacked using different Theatre of the Oppressed techniques. Rainbow of Desire and Cops-in-the-Head use Image Theatre to facilitate a sort of drama-therapy where internal struggles are externalized and confronted. This workbook doesn't go into detail about these techniques, but they are very helpful for theatrically exploring internalized oppression! More resources on this are in the Index of Tools.

Scenario 4: In the actor's story, we cannot tell if the Antagonist is an oppressor...

Does it work? Maybe

WHY?

Oppressive experiences can be confusing, so we get it. If this is a problem that is repeating in other places with other people, it's likely a problem worth investigating but let's ask a few follow-up questions: Even if the Antagonist isn't a gatekeeper, is it possible some type of power dynamics are at play here? What about structural privilege based on identities like race or class? Has the troupe identified all the power relations in the story?

Scenario 4A: Come to think of it, the Antagonist wasn't really in a more powerful position than the actor who told the story.

Does it work? No

WHY?

Well, it's possible that their story is about conflict, not oppression, so we'll say NO. And be very careful if your actor was in a more powerful position than their so-called Antagonist! For example, if they are a teacher with a story about not getting what they "needed" from their Black students who kept calling them "Whitey," the ethics of implying that the students are upholding an oppressive system are very questionable.

Scenario 4B: Sort of. I don't think it was the Antagonist's fault. I don't think she could have done anything more in that situation. I mean, she was just following the rules.

Does it work? Yes

WHY?

Hold up. Oppressors can be polite, passive, and complicit, and we are trained to give them the benefit of the doubt. Individuals don't have to be explicitly racist to be working for a racist system. We can and should interrogate their complicity and the policies they uphold on stage. So YES, let's Forum that story....

Scenario 4C: Well, the Antagonist was in a position of power but they also share the same identity as the Protagonist.

Does it work? Yes

WHY?

That happens sometimes. Just because a person is Black, for example, doesn't mean they can't uphold Anti-Blackness. This kind of a Forum Play could get very complicated but also very rich.

Finally, keep in mind that a group may not come into the process with a shared language or analysis of oppression and anti-oppression work. This is because most systems of oppression aren't obvious or visible. As a result, we're encouraged to assimilate, be complicit, and blame ourselves for our struggles. We recommend that Jokers stay alert during the rehearsal process, and ask a lot of questions (of themselves but also the troupe) to think through the stories that actors share. Continue to read critical texts, train in other anti-oppression practices and revisit this section to reflect on how you explore and understand what is being shared.

FROM REALITY TO STORY

It takes thoughtful facilitation to use individual stories as source material for playmaking and performing. Set the expectation that the play won't be one person's biography. Instead, it will reflect multiple experiences in the group. ✳

This means it might not portray a situation exactly as it happened. While the problems presented should be real, the specific facts of the Forum Scenes may not be true to life.

Let's say your troupe is working on oppression in the workplace. Fictionalizing details could look like...

* Naming a character Mr. White instead of using the name of someone's actual boss. (A small detail to highlight a racial dynamic.)
* Combining details about Antagonists from two different stories. For example, the story about the woman who was a micromanaging boss, and the story of the man who was a misogynistic teacher could become a play with an Antagonist who is a micromanaging and misogynistic boss! (A medium-sized detail to build solidarity.)
* Making a play about the undocumented experience of a man from Honduras who works at an auto shop, even though the story is based on the experiences of an undocumented woman from Nigeria who works at a restaurant. (Shifting many details to protect the actors.)

The group can show their care for the stories that are shared and not used, sometimes by simply thanking people for sharing. Jokers can also find creative ways to include these stories in the process, like a poem or a short interlude in the play.

Once the group decides the focus of their performance, the Jokers guide the process of generating scenes and outlining a "play." There are several ways that TONYC's Jokers and actors have put stories and scenes together. Each of these strategies has strengths and pitfalls:

USING ONE PERSON'S REAL-LIFE STORY
A series of scenes that focus on one person's experience

EXAMPLE

The play shows a woman struggling to keep custody of her son, while she lives with a boyfriend who isn't interested in helping her.

WAYS TO GET THERE

The group decides that an individual's story is compelling and wants to make the play about it. The actor who shared that story agrees.

PITFALLS

If other members of the group have limited experience in the situation, they may misrepresent it as they scene-build. There may be tension around deciding which details to include or not; the person who is the focus may struggle with the constant focus; it becomes difficult to rehearse if that person is absent.

STRENGTHS

The group can base all the content on the real-life events, and has clarity about what to represent.

USING EVERYONE'S STORY
A series of scenes that show an experience that everyone in the group has struggled with

EXAMPLE

A play shows a housing benefits office, where many characters struggle to get information about applications or updates to their applications from years ago.

WAYS TO GET THERE

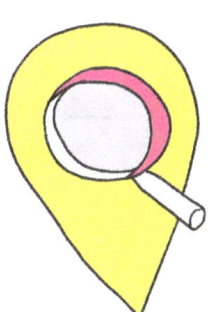

As the group shares stories, they realize they share a struggle and come up with a way to focus on one location or access point.

PITFALLS

It might be difficult to create a play that doesn't seem to be repeating the same scene multiple times.

STRENGTHS

The group experiences a strong sense of unity, bringing their own individual experiences into one play. This is an opportunity to really interrogate one system; it's easy to build comedic bits with "recurring" characters or gags.

MAKING A MASHUP
A Forum Play with two Protagonists whose stories coexist or are shown in alternating scenes. The problem in the stories has a shared root.

EXAMPLE

Two young people are struggling to get a job, and both apply for the same position. One is hired, but is sexually harassed through the hiring and onboarding process. The other is gender nonconforming, and the cis-gender interviewer inappropriately judges their appearance.

WAYS TO GET THERE

The group identifies a shared experience, and chooses to include scenes that show two specific versions.

PITFALLS

Creating completely imagined relationships to make two separate stories fit together may become messy or distract the focus from the central problems.

STRENGTHS

This model can highlight the role of an institution and its impact on many individuals. Especially if you have a bigger troupe, the play can depict how multiple instances of interpersonal oppression add up to create a larger systemic or institutional problem.

COLLAGING
A Forum presentation that includes a few distinct scenes, with different settings and Protagonists. These scenes may share a theme, like family, or a system, like Immigration.

EXAMPLE

A scene about a student getting suspended, followed by an employee experiencing racist comments at work, followed by someone who is undocumented and is denied treatment by an EMT.

WAYS TO GET THERE

A group has multiple stories that they want to show and represent.

PITFALLS

If the Forum Presentation doesn't include Interventions for each scene, then one group may feel like their problem didn't get support. It can also be harder to highlight how oppression is connected when the Protagonists aren't connected. The group may not build as much solidarity.

STRENGTHS

The group can assign actors based on which story they want to collaborate on. There is less pressure to devise one narrative.

As the actors hone in on what story or stories they want to stage, Jokers can start taking notes during rehearsal to make sure the problem of the Forum Play is clear. Things can get muddy when you start combining stories and details, so at the very least make doubly sure that your actors feel confident in their understanding of:

* Who is (are) the Protagonist(s) / Whose problem(s) are we trying to highlight in this Forum Play?
* What is it that the Protagonist(s) needs/need?
* What is the problem or failure they experience trying to access their human rights?
* Who is/are the Antagonist(s) or gatekeeper(s) that is/are denying the needs of the Protagonist?

Some light documentation will help remind actors from week to week or update actors who may have missed a rehearsal.

REVIEW YOUR NOTES

Ideally, Jokers start taking notes from Week 1 on themes, connections, and stories. Helping the actors hone in on which narrative to turn into a play may require that, between rehearsals, the Joker looks back at all the random ideas that have come up organically through Games, exercises, and initial improvisation. The Jokers can repeat back these ideas at key moments to prompt strong scene-building. Co-Jokers may also synthesize those ideas into a strong proposal for tying the experiences of the actors into one of these structures while encouraging actors to let go of any ideas that don't support the intentions of Forum Theatre.

To explore some of these ideas further, check out the worksheet "Jokers Have Stories Too" on p. 159 in the Index of Tools.

Notes

These pages are yours! Feel free to skip around, write in the margins, rip out pages, and add your own ideas!

ENGAGING SPECT-ACTORS

Chapter 6 includes some helpful activities that Jokers can use to prepare the troupe for the big day, including some handy flash cards for performance. You got this!

PREPARING YOUR ACTORS

Before the performance (around Week 8 or 9), a Joker should make sure the troupe actors really understand what will happen during the Forum. They particularly need to understand what happens after they present the play and how their responsibilities shift during the Interventions. They should also be prepared for the way the Joker will engage the audience during the show. Organizing a dress rehearsal in which a few invited guests are willing to become rehearsal Spect-Actors can help the troupe get used to the kind of improvisation that happens in the Forum.

If you can't find any invited guests, your actors can also pretend to be Spect-Actors for a rehearsal. Asking actors to play both their character and a Spect-Actor in the audience can be confusing but fun. Sometimes, a Joker can ask the actors to watch a scene they aren't in from the perspective of a potential audience member—perhaps their parents—and comment on the show the way their mama would, for instance.

When actors rehearse Forum Interventions, they often find it tempting to add their Interventions to the Forum Play, either by changing the ending, or showing the Protagonist trying many good ideas for solving the problem. During these rehearsals, you should edit to make the problem clearer, but remind everyone that they need to show the problem (not solutions), so that the audience is activated to try their own ideas.

Remind your troupe that during the upcoming Forum Play, Spect-Actors will be trying out new ideas to challenge the Antagonist and change the outcome of the play. All of the actors are responsible for portraying the reality of the systems of oppression in a way that can challenge these new ideas. (We don't want to oversimplify the solution to complicated problems!) The actor playing the Antagonist must have a sort of double consciousness. This actor knows how to stay in character, even if that means resisting change, while at the same time being a generous scene partner to the Spect-Actor.

The activity we call **Pushing Against** (see p. 200) is a metaphor for how the actor playing the Antagonist must listen to the Spect-Actor and make space for their idea, while giving them an equal amount of pushback with dialogue and action. Other actors may be called upon to play new characters (e.g., supervisors, cops, 911 operators, etc.) as well, so make sure your ensemble is ready to jump into the improvisation as needed.

It's especially important to distinguish between **Rehearsal Games** (p. 198), where you are exploring character choices in order to go back and make edits to the original Forum Play, and this **Intervention Prep** where you might see a good idea for solving the problem as you rehearse the Forum and Spect-Actor interactions. Going back to your original Forum Play and making edits that solve the problem or show the Protagonist trying too many tactics can leave your audience feeling uninspired or inactivated. So make sure that you're editing the original Forum Play only in order to make the problem clearer.

JOKER PREP

Just as actors get to rehearse every week, our co-Joker teams set aside 1-3 hours, about a week before a performance, to rehearse how they will facilitate the show. Jokers can do this during the regular rehearsal time, while the actors do their own Intervention Prep, or better yet, invite some other Joker Practitioners who can pretend to be audience members for a separate Joker rehearsal! Practice facilitating Interventions by creating a safe space for your pretend audience members to challenge your Jokering. You can simulate different challenges that may come up, like reluctant participation from the audience, victim-blaming, soap-boxing, or anything else that might happen in real life. Your peers should reflect back to you how your Jokering impacted them. (A framework for how to reflect on Joker practice is Chapter 7, on p. 122.)

Even if you're an experienced Joker, it's helpful to think through the challenges your specific play might encounter in a Forum. You'll be much more prepared to facilitate an ethical and robust conversation with the audience. This is also a great time to consider updating the Joker script or adjusting your Jokering style if you can predict that the audience or even the content of the play might need something a little different than your default style.

One of our go-to tactics when an Intervention or statement feels judgy or misplaced is to ask a question. For example, asking "How easy is it for everyone to...bring a parent to speak to the principal on their behalf?" might be a gentle way to check the privilege of someone well-intentioned who might not be aware of the realities of students living with single, working parents. However, if you have an audience member that's spouting generalizations about undocumented people sneaking across the border and avoiding taxes, you could shift attention back to the actors. Asking questions like "Are there other ways that immigrants end up undocumented in this country?" or "How likely is it that this character

Four tips for "shy" audiences that are hesitant to intervene in a Forum

If they've already been given some time to brainstorm an idea with their neighbor and you've really clarified the instructions...

Wait

Give them some silence and let it be uncomfortable. This is a moment of good confusion!

Positive Encouragement

Look for the person in the crowd who is clearly considering coming up. Maybe they didn't raise their hand but their shoulders are wiggling in a way that indicates they might have an idea. Get the audience to clap and encourage them to be a brave Spect-Actor!

Guilt Trip

Lean into the solidarity we built and then ask "Do we really want these problems to stay the same?" or "Are we saying these problems can't change?"

Plant

Have someone in the audience who is prepared to be the first volunteer.

Make It Exciting

After a first Intervention, give the audience some new ideas for their second and third Interventions. They can bring a friend. Invent a new scene or character. Or even do a quick policy brainstorm.

would have been paying taxes?" can help open up the discussion, but keep it grounded in our shared values.

During the Forum (between the play and the intervention) is often when victim-blaming pops up from the audience which means there is an opportunity for the Joker to challenge that mindset. Depending on how you ask the questions, one Spect-Actor might say, "I think it's a problem that Kendra was so rude to her teacher!" Can you invite another spect-actor to challenge that thinking? Try to ask a follow-up question, "Did anyone catch why or when Kendra started getting rude with her teacher?" This might remind folks of other subtle injustices that had been ignored. (For more tips about this tricky part of the Joker script and ideas for what questions to ask your audience, jump to the Joker Flash Card on "Identifying the Problems" p. 105)

So much can happen in the Forum that it's important for Jokers to rehearse the Forum as well as the play to prepare for different kinds of audience interactions. At TONYC, Jokers practice responses to offensive comments that range from gentle questions that highlight an audience member's unconscious bias to a conversation smackdown.

Your goal isn't to call out Spect-Actors.

Your facilitation of the Intervention should ideally call in Spect-Actors to take collective action in solidarity with the actors.

JOKER SCRIPT FLASH CARDS

Joker script intentions

Our Joker Script Flash Cards were created to refresh the memory of Jokers who are still learning what the ingredients of a Forum are. This section explains how to use the Joker script and how you can adapt it to make your own.

BEFORE THE PLAY STARTS

WARM UP

INTO AND OUT OF THE PLAY

IDENTIFYING THE PROBLEMS

SOLIDARITY BUILDING

ACTIVATING SPECT-ACTORS TO INTERVENE

GETTING SPECT-ACTOR READY TO INTERVENE

DURING THE INTERVENTION

POST-INTERVENTION QUESTIONS

You can cut out these cards to use during your performance! Flip each card for more information!

BEFORE THE PLAY STARTS

Before the play starts

How do you want to welcome your audience? Do you want to immerse them theatrically into the problem before you've even said hello? How much do you want to explain to the audience about how Forum Theatre works before they experience it? TONYC Jokers tend to simply let our audiences know that they are not just spectators but rather Spect-Actors here. We allow them to watch the rest unfold moment by moment.

BEFORE THE PLAY STARTS

DO:
Introduce yourself and the troupe/project.
Thank the space, partners, etc.

SAY (SOMETHING LIKE): "Do you all have any problems?
We have problems too. We don't want these problems to
stay the same. We want to take action. That's where you
come in. You're not just spectators, you're Spect-Actors.
And like the actors, it's time to warm up."

TIP(S):
Always transition us to the next part.

Warm up

The main thing that the Joker is trying to de-mechanize here is the traditional relationship between audiences and actors. This is how you start to create the Spect-Actor. It really helps if the audience can see from the beginning that we don't expect them to just sit back and watch the show. It doesn't really matter what Game you use to prepare them for the Interventions to come, but your audience should feel ready to dialogue with each other, problem solve together, and use their bodies and voices to take action.

WARM UP

DO: De-mechanize their minds and prepare their bodies to take action.

EXAMPLES:

Handshake Game

Two people shake hands but can't let go until both people are holding other hands.

Yes/No Game

* Use simple opposites like, yes/no, up/down, left/right.
* Start with simple patterns like "yes, yes, no" (audience says "no, no, yes.")
* Mix it up, going from easy to hard: "yes, up, left" (audience says "no, down, right.")

SAY (SOMETHING LIKE): "Now that we're a bit confused, we're ready to look at these problems in a new way!"

INTO AND OUT OF THE PLAY

Into and out of the play

Getting the audience to say '3, 2, 1, Action"
collectively is arguably part of their warm up. Again,
they should use their voices and collective power
to initiate something. This frame around the play
reminds us that this performance is still a rehearsal
for real life. While the play is happening, the Joker
should be present, watching to see if the actors need
any support. Finally, after the play, the actors should
bow and receive applause.

It's important that the actors get a chance to step
away from their characters for emotional well-being
and/or to tend to their psychological health, and to
remind themselves and the audience that this is still
theatre. Sometimes the actors may need a break

INTO AND OUT OF THE PLAY

DO:
Make sure the actors are ready, then get the audience to say: "3, 2, 1, ACTION."

Observe the play.

Audience should applaud.

Actors may bow and fully introduce themselves with pronouns.

Actors should rearrange themselves so that the Joker can talk to the audience.

Into and out of the play (cont.)

during the show, but they also have a responsibility to engage with the audience during the Forum, and the Joker may need to navigate that tension.

Remind your actors to stay present on stage for the next part of the dialogue, if possible. While the actors should make space for the audience's ideas, a Joker might call upon the actors to fact-check or even privilege-check. Any actor playing an Antagonist should be engaged in this dialogue (mostly as a listener) so they can prepare for Interventions with Spect-Actors.

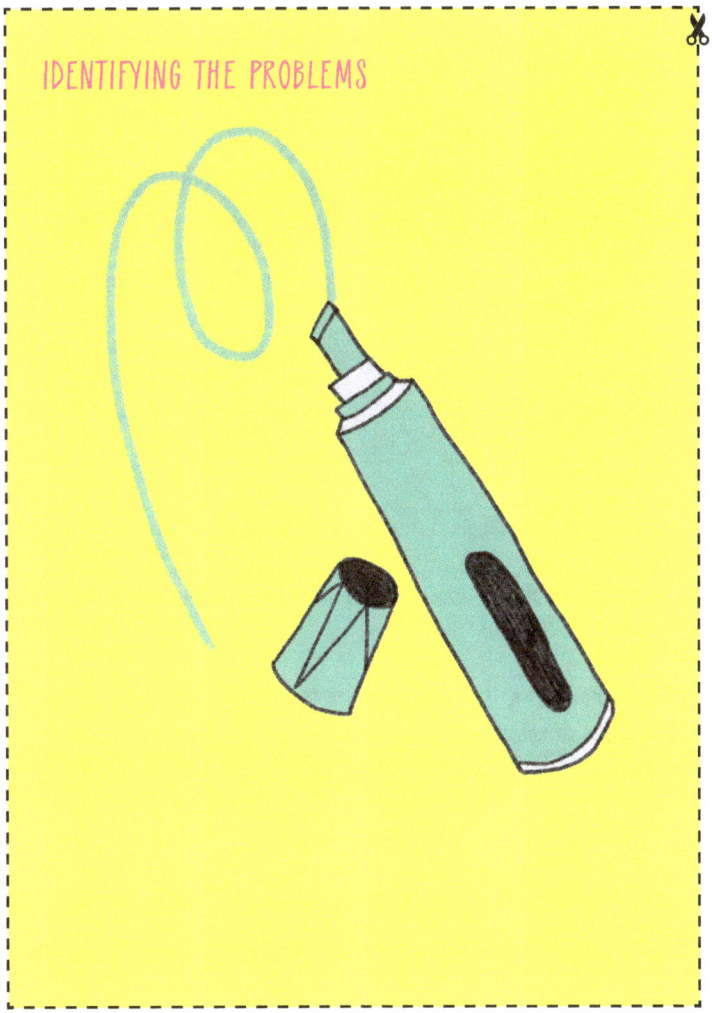

IDENTIFYING THE PROBLEMS

Identifying the problems

Do we really need to name the problems if we have made a strong Forum Play? Absolutely!

We shouldn't assume that everyone views oppression in the same way. One Spect-Actor may shout out, "I saw racism!" The Joker should then interrogate a bit, "Say more. Where did you see the characters facing racism?" Hopefully the Spect-Actor is able to specify something like "It was racist when the teacher touched Kendra's braids without asking for permission." This helps ensure that the whole audience is able to connect singular events and interactions to larger patterns and cultures of oppression and harm.

IDENTIFYING THE PROBLEMS

SAY (SOMETHING LIKE):
"Did you see the main character(s) facing any problems?"

"Do you see these problems happen in the world around you?"

TIP(S):
If the audience does not mention a problem, offer prompts "What about when they _____?"

Get specific moments in the play when they saw it.

If the audience doesn't know if these problems happen in real life, ask the actors.

Start to read the audience for things like: accessibility, who's speaking the most in the room, the energy.

This is also an opportunity for the Joker to clarify whose problem we are here to solve. In other words, to make sure everyone understands whose side we are on. If there is bad confusion about this, the Forum should not press on. Sometimes it helps to name the oppressed characters early on in this section e.g., "What problems did we see our main character Kendra, facing?". Just like you may have asked your troupe when you were developing themes for your play, at this moment you can ask the audience to name what the Protagonist needed that they could not attain.

Remember, if the audience isn't getting something, you can turn to your actors for their perspectives.

SOLIDARITY BUILDING

Solidarity building

We include this part of the script to give the audience a chance to check their privilege and relationship to the problem. The specific oppression depicted may feel unfamiliar to them, but they may have empathy for the more general experience of being denied by a person or system that was supposed to help. Try to give three prompts (ranging from specific to broad) that will get the majority of the group to relate in some way. This will help to encourage the Spect-Actors to invest in the collective brainstorming to come, in solidarity with the actors.

SOLIDARITY BUILDING

SAY (SOMETHING LIKE): "Raise your hand if:"

* "You've experienced this problem / a problem you saw."
* "You've experienced something like the problem."
* "You've ever felt what this character was feeling."
* "You've been unable to get something you needed because of who you are, or who people think you are."

"Thank you. So, we here know something about these problems."

SAMPLE SOLIDARITY PROMPTS FROM SPECIFIC TO BROAD:
"Raise your hand if you attended a school like 'Hostile High' where people in power treated you and people that looked like you as criminals."

"Maybe your school wasn't like Hostile High but can you also raise your hand if you've ever been accused of something you didn't do and gotten in trouble? Maybe at school or work?"

"Now raise a hand if you have ever gone to someone who you thought would help you and you felt like they just didn't see you."

ACTIVATING SPECT-ACTORS TO INTERVENE

Activating Spect-Actors to intervene

Another favorite practice we have found is giving the audience some time (between 30 and 120 seconds) to talk through their idea with the people around them first. If you're rushed for time, you can shorten or cut this part, but this is a good time to warn your audience of what's to come and your intentions: "We don't have to solve the problem. Neither are we here to blame the victim for their own oppression. We're here to practice taking action and prepare for the next time this happens."

Interventions can make people feel exposed, so processing in pairs or in a small group is another way to warm up Spect-Actors that are intimidated by acting or public speaking. Eventually, you'll need to

ACTIVATING SPECT-ACTORS TO INTERVENE

SAY (SOMETHING LIKE):
* "Turn to your neighbor and discuss what you might try if you were in the main character's shoes."

* "Now you have two ideas. You're not off the hook. Who has an idea? Who would like to try out an idea?"

* "Don't tell us! Come try it!"

TIP(S):
Have the Protagonist come to front of stage with their costume/prop to give to the Spect-Actor.

get your first Spect-Actor up on stage. There may be some reluctance, but don't give up!

Visit p. 97 for more tips on activating shy or reluctant audiences.

GETTING SPECT-ACTORS READY TO INTERVENE

Getting Spect-Actors ready to intervene

Now that you have a willing participant, you should support their participation in a few ways:

* Ask for names and pronouns—Aside from being courteous and welcoming, you can't underestimate the importance of letting the Spect-Actor introduce themselves. The grammar of the Forum gets tricky when you have a specific Spect-Actor playing a character who has their own identity (as in their own name and pronouns). This will help your other audience members respect the humanity of both entities and you can model this later by saying things like, "This version of Rakim, which was played by Alanna: what did he try?"

GETTING SPECT-ACTORS READY TO INTERVENE

SAY (SOMETHING LIKE):

* "Would you tell us your name and which pronouns we can use to talk about you after your done with this intervention?"

* "What moment do you want to take it from?"

TIP(S):

You may have to provide an example of your pronouns.

Make sure they are stepping in as a Protagonist or appropriate ally. Intervening as an Antagonist is not allowed. If that wasn't their original idea, ask if they can try their idea from the Protagonist's shoes or someone already allied with them and say something like, "Will pretending that the Antagonist is different prepare us for next time we're in the Protagonist's shoes?"

Continue to thank your Spect-Actor throughout the Intervention—when they first come up, after they intervene, and to send them offstage once the debrief of the Intervention is done.

* Especially, once they are on stage, the Spect-Actors are going to try to explain their idea with words. Please avoid this if possible and get them to say the bare minimum so that your actors can jump into the scene. This rule can be bent in some circumstances, for instance when your Spect-Actor has an idea for a new scene with a new character.

* You can save time by getting the Spect-Actor to be specific about where in the play they would like to intervene. There's no need to start the whole play over from the beginning or re-enact bits that aren't about the Spect-Actor's new idea. Also, while one Joker supports the Spect-Actor, the other can make sure the actors (especially the Antagonist) are ready to jump back in and engage

with this Spect-Actor's new idea.

* There are some T.O. practitioners who never allow someone of a different identity to intervene in a play that is about issues that only people of that identity face. For instance, a play that is specifically about the challenges of a Black, transgender woman might only allow Spect-Actors who are also Black, woman of trans experience to intervene. At TONYC, we strive for thoughtful audience curation but tend not to be as rigid about the Forum itself. Instead, we choose to remind each Spect-Actor that the Antagonist will be treating them as if they were a Black, transgender woman, in this case. This should not, in any way, encourage Spect-Actors to portray the Protagonist in a way that leans on stereotypes. In fact, it helps for them to be themselves. (This also opens up conversations later about the privilege
it takes to be calm or to have access to certain information.) This is really about the other actors reminding this new Spect-Actor of their reality and given circumstances.

* The Joker is not here to judge how the oppressed solve their problems (remember the story of Boal and the Landless Farmers, on p. 18). This means we are open to any Intervention, including one that portrays violence against the oppressor. We still have to keep our actors safe, though, which means telling the Spect-Actor that physical contact should be mimed or initiated very slowly so the actors have time to react and consent or play along. Some Spect-Actors get really into it so be careful to remind them this is still pretend! #DontHurtNobody

Notes

These pages are
yours! Feel free to
skip around, write
in the margins, rip
out pages, and add
your own ideas!

DURING THE INTERVENTION

During the Intervention

Again, this is all one giant rehearsal for the revolution. So don't be afraid to stop the Intervention if it's going off the rails. Sometimes Spect-Actors have bad confusion about what they're supposed to do or which character they are talking to. You can pause, re-explain, and start again.

Sometimes Spect-Actors bring up an idea that requires a brand new character. For example, a Spect-Actor starts the Intervention and asks to speak to the caseworker's supervisor. This is totally normal. You've already coached the actors to be ready to step into new roles that might exist in that institution or space. In this example, a Joker can help prompt an actor to jump in as the supervisor

DO:
Keep an eye out for what changed in the situation and/or Antagonist.

Look for pitfalls and opportunities and think about follow-up questions.

End the scene when the idea is complete, or audience starts looking at the Joker.

who was eavesdropping down the hall.

This is not "perfect" theatre. This is theatre that you create in front of the audience in real time. It can be messy and exciting. The Joker as a wild card may even jump in as an actor and bring their expertise to the dialogue.

After the Intervention

The intention here is to make sure we have all learned something from the Intervention. When we ask "What changed?" we are interested in even subtle differences in behavior by the Antagonist. Perhaps they seemed a little caught off guard. Great! That's information about the system we can use in the fight against oppression. When we ask "Would this work for everyone?" we are looking to identify certain privileges that make it easier to navigate this particular system of oppression. Asking "What might happen next?" is about assessing risk, especially if the Intervention was violent or disruptive. This is not a part of the "Joker Script" to be memorized but an attempt to facilitate the most robust conversation possible about the positives and negatives of new

POST-INTERVENTION QUESTIONS

SAY (SOMETHING LIKE):
* "What did they try?"
* "What changed?"
* "Would this work for everyone?"
* "What might happen next?"

TIP(S):
Joker is not there to answer these questions, but to ask and to explore the audience's answers. Avoid elaborating on/adding your own thoughts to what audience members say in response to the Intervention.

Fact Check—in case we need to get more information.

Get specific. Just respond to what that person did.

When someone starts giving another idea, get them up to try it.

Aim for at least three Interventions.

tactics. This is why watching the Intervention is key. You have to be curious about every aspect of the scene to make this part of the Forum feel like a meaty, educational discussion.

Wrapping up
When concluding a performance, you may encounter feelings of frustration, or uncertainty, or excitement, or all of these and more. That's great! There usually isn't a simple solution to these issues. The whole point of these performances is to spark discussions that lead to collective action.

You can always say something like, "We haven't found the one solution. Please continue the conversation inside and outside the theatre."

And finally, if you didn't thank the venue or the partners at the top of the performance, do it here! Acknowledge the actors again and encourage folks to stay in touch.

BEYOND THE FORUM

Chapter 7 goes deeper into the
work of continuously reflecting
on our Joker practice.

EVALUATING OUR JOKER PRACTICE

A Joker's facilitation sets the tone for rehearsals, workshops, and public shows. We've developed a framework for reflecting on facilitation so that Jokers can become more aware of the impact of their actions. With this information, Jokers can then adjust their facilitation to support the intentions of the collaborative space. At TONYC, Jokers gather for regular practice sessions in which they can reflect on their own work, and get feedback from colleagues and actors. In order to consistently and objectively evaluate Jokering, this framework looks at facilitation from three perspectives: accuracy, style, and ethics. These are the terms that TONYC uses, and they don't have to be your words. But the ideas they represent are key to improving and honing our Joker practices. Our definitions of these words are as follows:

Accuracy. In rehearsal and performance, we define *accuracy* as how clearly the facilitation guided the participants to the intended goals of the activity. This deserves particular attention in T.O., because many Games are intended to create "good confusion" that helps question and challenge our social norms. When our instructions are vague and inaccurate, participants can feel distracted, unsafe, and unsure of how to engage with the activity. That's what we call "bad confusion." When this happens, the boundaries of the exercise are unclear.

When the instructions and intentions of the activity are explicit, and the duration and order of the steps are appropriate, we play together, experience surprises together, and enter "good confusion." The group can then reflect on how the activity worked to warm them up, and the Joker can use the exercise as a metaphor to discuss real-life experiences. Similarly, in the performance, the Joker is responsible for making sure that the problems posed in the Forum Play are clear to the audience and that the rules of the Forum are understood as well. This supports the actors and Spect-Actors to improvise with a shared understanding.

Example

In the Game Boal calls *The Opposite of Jackson* (see p. 173), the facilitator asks participants to do the opposite of what the facilitator says. So if they tell people to look up, people should actually look down. This opens the space for participants to talk about how hard it is to change something we are programmed to know. To support everyone playing with the same rules, the facilitator can review specific opposites, like "walk/stop." If a facilitator gives an instruction that's too open-ended, like "Whatever I say, do the opposite: stop!" participants can interpret different opposites (go, walk, run) or may not know what to do at all.

WATCH YOUR LANGUAGE

Context impacts accuracy, so it may look different for different groups. Facilitating a Game in front of a group of facilitators with expertise in theatre is different from facilitating a group of participants with no theatre experience. Be mindful of your assumptions of what this group already knows. Are you using jargon like "pop-corn style" or "tableaux" without defining what those words mean? Inaccessible vocabulary can also lead to bad confusion.

Example

Jing may bring humor into the rehearsal room that keeps things fun and positive. However, if her intention is to manage some conflict resolution between actors, her dry wit may distance people who are feeling vulnerable or sensitive. She may want to identify a moment in which to find a slower, warm style in order to support the conversation and have a healing impact.

Style. *Style* includes the personal and distinct qualities of expression that a facilitator brings into the room. We invite Jokers to think about their style as something that's not static but fluid: capable of shifting and being de-mechanized to make sure their impact matches their intent. A Joker's style can be energetic, chill, severe, bubbly, teacherly, etc. These characteristics can motivate or distance a group in different ways, depending on the energy of the group at the moment, the point of the rehearsal process, etc. We encourage Jokers to try to describe style without judging different styles as "good or bad," but instead, to consider the impact that style can have on participants and an activity. We also need to consider that interpretations of particular styles can be connected to stereotypes based on race, gender identity, or class. When a facilitator reviews the perceptions of their style, they can decide to turn up or turn down specific elements in order to best support the needs of the activity and their relationship to the group.

Ethics. We reflect on the ethics of our practice by paying attention to the ways our facilitation uses tactics of oppressive systems (it does), as well as how our facilitation moves individuals and groups towards liberation. This could be about how the Joker considers access, consent, intentions, trauma, or cultural sensitivity. It could be about the Joker's understanding of "problem-posing education," and their role as a question-asker and learner, alongside the group. This also requires an awareness of the power dynamics in the room, including the facilitator's use of their power. Are there boundaries that support the group in playing Games as well as in the general community agreements? Is there too much permissiveness that adds confusion or harm?

Very often accuracy and style impact ethics. For example, if a Joker's style is teacherly, they may ask questions that don't leave space for learning or critical thinking, like: "Didn't we think this Game showed how power can be violent?" versus "What did this Game reveal about power, to you?" If a Joker's style is always bubbly, they may struggle to acknowledge and make space for trauma as it surfaces in the storytelling and scene-building. The ethics will shift depending on the cultural context of the group.

For more tools on evaluating your Joker practice, check out the following worksheets in the Index of Tools: "Event Self-Reflection, Accuracy/Style/Ethics" (p. 162) and "Personal-Style Deep Dive" (p. 164).

Notes

These pages are yours! Feel free to skip around, write in the margins, rip out pages, and add your own ideas!

GOING FURTHER

So you've made it this far! By this point, you may
have successfully completed a Forum Theatre
performance with a group of actors and you're all
looking for ways to take the collective action one
step further. The final section of this workbook
provides a blueprint for turning some of the ideas
you generated during the Forum Theatre Performance
into actionable policy demands through a process
called Legislative Theatre.

The Index presents a series of tools like a glossary,
step-by-step activities, and resources for further
reading. Remember, Jokering is a constant and
evolving practice. Let's get into it!

8. LEGISLATIVE THEATRE
9. CONCLUSION – REMEMBER THE REVOLUTION
10. INDEX OF TOOLS

LEGISLATIVE THEATRE

Chapter 8 introduces the Legislative Theatre process and some examples of times when it might be a helpful tool for your group.

WHAT'S LEGISLATIVE THEATRE?

The Legislative Theatre process is an option for developing a Forum Theatre play further. Plays presented in a Legislative Theatre process should focus on problems related to policies and rules within institutions or governments, like the injustice of the cash bail system, for instance.

Just like Forum Theatre, Legislative Theatre presents an original play. But this play specifically depicts the bureaucracy and power structures of an oppressive institution. Legislative Theatre also involves Forum Interventions. But after the Interventions, Spect-Actors, advocates, and decision makers collaborate on coming up with specific and feasible policy proposals. These proposals can:

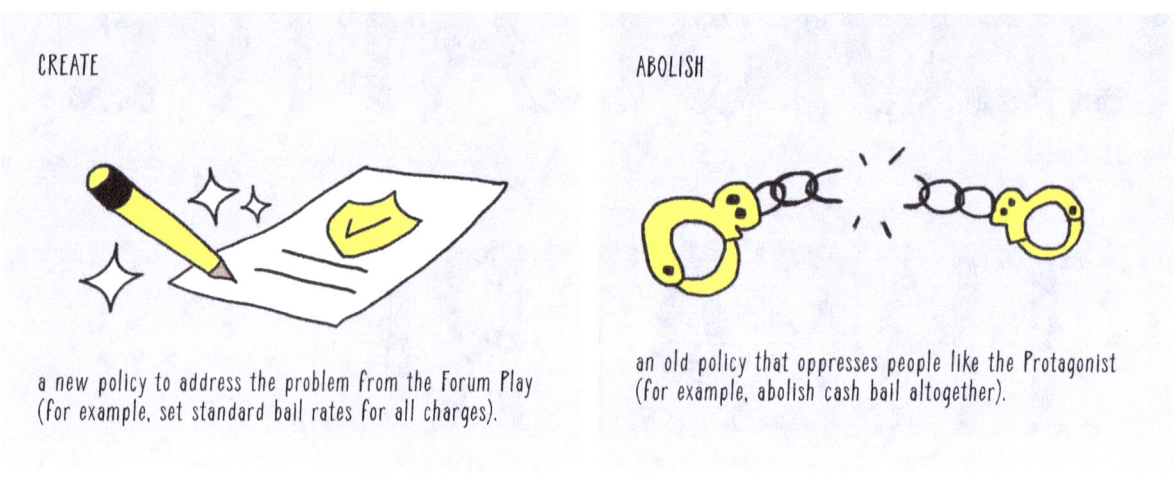

CREATE

a new policy to address the problem from the Forum Play (for example, set standard bail rates for all charges).

ABOLISH

an old policy that oppresses people like the Protagonist (for example, abolish cash bail altogether).

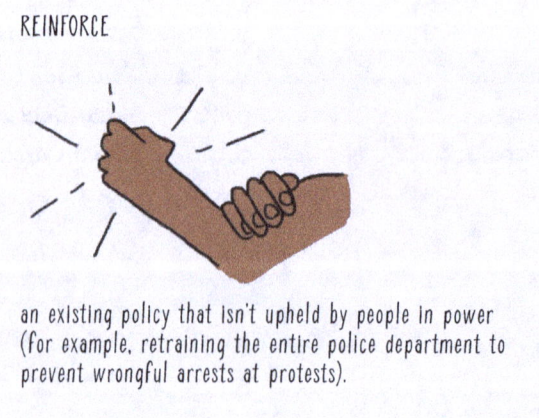

REINFORCE

an existing policy that isn't upheld by people in power (for example, retraining the entire police department to prevent wrongful arrests at protests).

To be clear, we're not just talking about changing laws and legislation: we mean any rules, practices, or unspoken norms that impact human lives. This could be about changing human resource (HR) guidelines to make it easier to report abuse in the workplace, or even updating training for public transportation staff so that they are equipped to interrupt sexual harassment. When we talk about changing rules, we need to look at rules that are already in place but aren't effectively or ethically implemented, or haven't been implemented at all!

To influence structural change and generate better, more equitable rules through Legislative Theatre, you'll need to build effective and collaborative partnerships. You'll need all the people who are impacted by those rules and laws to be in your audience. This is true for any Forum event, and especially true for Legislative Theatre. Your audience should include:

People who have experienced what the actors show on stage

Organizers and advocacy groups

Decision makers and legislators, like local elected officials

READY FOR LEGISLATIVE THEATRE?

Your Forum Play might be ripe for Legislative Theatre if rules are a central theme. This might become apparent when…

* The troupe is telling their personal stories where they couldn't get what they needed from the "gatekeeper," not (just) because of what the Antagonist thought about them but because of rules that were racist, sexist, or homophobic, etc.

* Moments of "crisis" that focus on individual interactions seem decentered in your play. Instead, the play focuses on problems that reveal bureaucracy—rules that don't allow people in power (even nice gatekeepers) to change a situation to meet someone's needs.

* The play wants to move up the power chain. If the character in the story confronts a gatekeeper, like a nurse, do we meet any other characters that the nurse reports to? Do we find out what pressures the nurse faces that impact their ability to respond to the needs of the character? Plays with scenes with managers or supervisors are great for Legislative Theatre. Often when people are dealing with an institution, the frontline staff person they are interacting with isn't the person with the most power. Sometimes, the frontline staff person has have very little concrete power in the institution.

Here's an example of the kind of story Legislative Theatre can tell

Hayden, a first-generation Jamaican-American and his best friend from work attend a Black Lives Matter protest together while they are furloughed from their restaurant job during the pandemic. Despite being lawfully present, they are both arrested. Hayden's best friend, who is white and economically privileged, is able to call his parents to pay his $5,000 bail for release but Hayden, who has no safety net, isn't able to pay his $10,000 bail and loses his apartment while he awaits trial. Hayden never recovers from this encounter with the criminal justice system—financially, socially, or professionally—and is arrested 30 years later for stealing groceries, only to discover his old friend has become a judge.

GETTING CONSENT

Talk about using the Legislative Theatre process with the community actors from the beginning. How do folks feel about local politics in your area? What are their relationships with elected officials? For some folks, the idea of influencing local politics is exciting; for others, it can be frustrating, intimidating, or simply feel like a waste of time. Before moving forward, make sure the troupe is on board!

RESEARCH

The troupe may need to research in order to develop scenes between the frontline staff and their superiors and clarify the levels of bureaucracy that the Protagonists are up against. If there's no information available about the power chain in this situation, then this lack might be reflected in the play too. For example, the character may ask to see the supervisor, but they're blocked from knowing the identity or even existence of a supervisor. That lack of transparency may be a policy problem in itself.

This research should be a collective process. Use the Internet; ask people who work in the institutions; or call the decision makers and advocates whom you've already invited to be a part of the performance. At every rehearsal, identify questions about HOW and WHY things are happening.

WHAT DOES LEGISLATIVE THEATRE LOOK LIKE?

When TONYC started experimenting with Legislative Theatre in 2013, we created a tagline: **#WatchActVote.** You already know how to **#Watch** a Forum Play and **#Act** out Interventions from the Forum Theatre process, so now you're almost there!

After the last Intervention, audience members are invited to compose policy ideas on slips of paper. These are read, sorted, and processed by the decision makers, during the event.

#Vote is the final part of our Legislative Theatre events. The decision makers or legislators present the actors and audience with up to three policy proposals based on the collected ideas. After each group presents their proposal, the Joker opens the floor for points of clarification, disagreements (dissent), and changes (amendments). Proposals can be clarified or amended based on the debate.

Everyone who is present at the performance votes on the proposals. The legislators or decision makers are expected to commit to taking one or more action steps to carry forward any proposals that have passed the community voting process.

ACTIONS AFTER THE SHOW

Many follow-up actions can help to deepen the creative advocacy after the Legislative Theatre event. These may include:

* Policy negotiation meetings with people in power, and specifically with the decision makers who participated in the event.

* Rallies or protests.

* Social media campaigns directed at participating decision makers.

* Workshops on participatory democracy.

* Joining existing campaign efforts led by local, grassroots organizations.

* The important thing is to have a thorough follow-up plan ahead of time, in hopes that the ideas that are generated don't get forgotten or ignored.

Our concrete successes in Legislative Theatre have included:

Municipal ID

In a 2014 event, a TONYC play portrayed a transgender woman who experienced domestic violence and ended up getting arrested instead of being protected. In the Forum Play, when the police arrived, they accused her of holding fake identification because the gender marker on her ID didn't match her name and presentation. In attendance was Council Member Carlos Menchaca, whose Municipal ID bill was in development. The Forum improvisations led to the proposal that the new ID should allow applicants to (1) state their preferred gender marker without having to show proof of medical procedures, or (2) leave the gender box blank. This became part of the bill voted through by City Council later in 2014. Menchaca says that this play shaped his thinking.

Cultural Plan

During the development of NYC's first Cultural Plan in 2017, TONYC actors with experience of homelessness performed a play about their work as artists, and their systemic exclusion from the traditional cultural sector. A scene about artists facing arrest for vending art in the park led participating Council Member Stephen Levin to introduce new legislation to increase the historically low number of street vendor licenses issued by the city. Additional policy proposals, like a hotline of resources for artists being targeted by law enforcement, were integrated into the Cultural Plan.

NYC Community Safety Act

In 2013, a group of trans youth made a Forum Play with TONYC about the impact of a discriminatory practice by the New York City Police Department, in which the possession of three or more condoms could be viewed as evidence of prostitution. The scene in which the young people were violently stopped, searched, and then arrested on suspicion of prostitution was developed in conjunction with an ongoing campaign by many organizations called "No Condoms as Evidence." NYC Council Member Jimmy Van Bramer was in attendance, and stated that the play influenced his vote on the NYC Community Safety Act later that year, aimed at ending discriminatory policing. In 2014, as a result of extensive advocacy and campaigning, NYC then announced it would stop using condoms as evidence.

HASA Housing Vouchers and the NYC Council

In 2017, the TONYC Housing Works Troupe created a play based on their experiences facing illegal discrimination from landlords and forced evictions, due to being HASA (HIV/AIDS Services Administration) voucher holders. The HASA program paid the tenants' rent directly to landlords, in two installments each month. Some landlords were then claiming that the tenants were late with half their rent, although this arrangement was mandated by the State. Following the Forum Play, NYC Council staff met repeatedly with Housing Works members to understand the bureaucratic issue, and escalated the issue to New York State policymakers.

For more stories of Legislative Theatre, feedback from advocates and legislators who participated, and the tangible outcomes that resulted, check out TONYC's "Report on Legislative Theatre Policy and Civic Engagement Impact," written in 2017 by Rebecca Kelly-Golfman.

This is only a taste of what Legislative Theatre has looked like for us at TONYC. We hope to bring you more content about this branch of Theatre of the Oppressed in the years to come. And just as with all Theatre of the Oppressed work, Legislative Theatre is an ever-evolving practice! Use your creativity to refine and adapt the process to meet the needs of the communities you work with. So whether you're starting with Legislative Theatre Version 1 or Version 100, we encourage you and your collaborators to keep experimenting!

To explore some of these ideas further, check out "Are You Ready to Make Your Forum Play into Legislative Theatre?" on p. 170 in the Index of Tools.

REMEMBER THE REVOLUTION

p. 140 *Conclusion*

CONCLUSION

We believe in Forum Theatre as a way to rehearse for reality. We prepare to take action by testing alternatives in real time and assessing the pitfalls and successes in the concrete actions our community tried. As a whole, Theatre of the Oppressed was developed as a tool to change systems of oppression. The cycle of action and reflection is central to most of the tools, and it's important for a Joker to apply that cycle to their own developing practice. We learned most of what we know about Jokering from doing it. And repeating it. And learning from our mistakes. And trying out new ideas. And feeling what happened in the room. And going back to our notes when we got lost. And watching others. And learning more about the world. And Jokering again.

This text is a beginning, a place to return to, another tool that invites action and reflection. In *Pedagogy of the Oppressed,* Paulo Freire says that dialogue needs love, humility, faith, trust, hope and critical thinking. While the words we've written can't replace the cycles that you will experience to develop your practice, this workbook intends to be a fun, rigorous, and joyful companion. We're glad you're on the journey with us as we succeed and stumble together!

Finally, the experience of Jokering, when we engage in the cycle of action and reflection, is transformative. There's a vast spectrum of experiences that collide as we share and create, so reflection can also be a way to tell your own story along the way.

We hope this workbook supports your exploration, that you come back to it when needed, and that you share your ideas and learnings with other Jokers—us included.

Let's go: 3, 2, 1, Action!

Notes

These pages are
yours! Feel free to
skip around, write
in the margins, rip
out pages, and add
your own ideas!

INDEX OF TOOLS

GLOSSARY

Actor
A person collaborating in a troupe to create and perform a play based on the troupe members' lived experiences of oppression; "actors" seek to challenge that oppression through theatre and action.

Antagonist
The character(s) in the play who creates or upholds the obstacle that is preventing the Protagonist from obtaining what they need. Sometimes called gatekeeper or oppressor.

Forum Play
A play about an oppressed person(s) that ends with the Protagonist not getting what they need. The unsatisfying ending of this play inspires a subsequent "Forum" or community brainstorming session about solutions to the presented problem.

Forum Theatre
The technique of using a play about a real-life, unresolved problem to generate dialogue and strategies to fight oppression via interactive theatre.

Intervention
The process of a Spect-Actor entering into the play that is facilitated by actors and Jokers.

Joker
Facilitators of the play-creation process and public performance; like the Joker in a deck of cards, they do not belong to any particular suit.

Legislative Theatre
An extension of Forum Theatre that uses both the problems of the Forum Play and the dialogue and strategies explored in the Forum to inspire a community to collaborate on changing the laws, policies, and rules that allowed the characters in the play to face oppression or injustice.

Oppression

A person or a community being exploited or blocked from their human rights, including the right to express their own identity.

Protagonist

The character(s) in the play who faces an oppressive obstacle in obtaining what they need.

Spect-Actors

Audience members who jump into the play and act out potential strategies for change or brainstorm about tactics to fight the oppression in the play.

Theatre of the Oppressed (T.O.) versus Theatre of the Oppressed NYC (TONYC)

T.O. is a set of activities that is practiced around the world, started by Augusto Boal. TONYC is an organization based in NYC that practices T.O. So we pronounce it: tee-oh-en-why-see.

TREE OF THEATRE OF THE OPPRESSED

Roots

Word, Sound, and Image. These are weapons that are used against us (tying back to programming, mechanizing) that we can use in our fight: they are also elements of theatre. This is why the theatre is an incredible tool for fighting oppression.

Nutrients

Feeding the roots. History, ethics, solidarity, economy, philosophy, and politics: we must learn these and use them to our advantage in the fight.

Games/Exercises

We use these to de-mechanize, to be able to identify and begin to change the problems. We must de-mechanize physically and mentally. This HAS to be the first step.

Four categories of games for de-mechanization
1. See everything we look at.
2. Listen to all that we hear.
3. Feel all that we touch.
4. Stimulate various senses.

Image Theatre

Identify, share the problem. Communicate without the confusion of words, at the early stages of forming a collective to initiate change.

Forum Theatre

Bring the problem to the community, in the form of a play, and invite Interventions and alternatives onstage.

All of this is leading to concrete and ethical social actions. This is the goal of T.O., which must always be the most important intention.

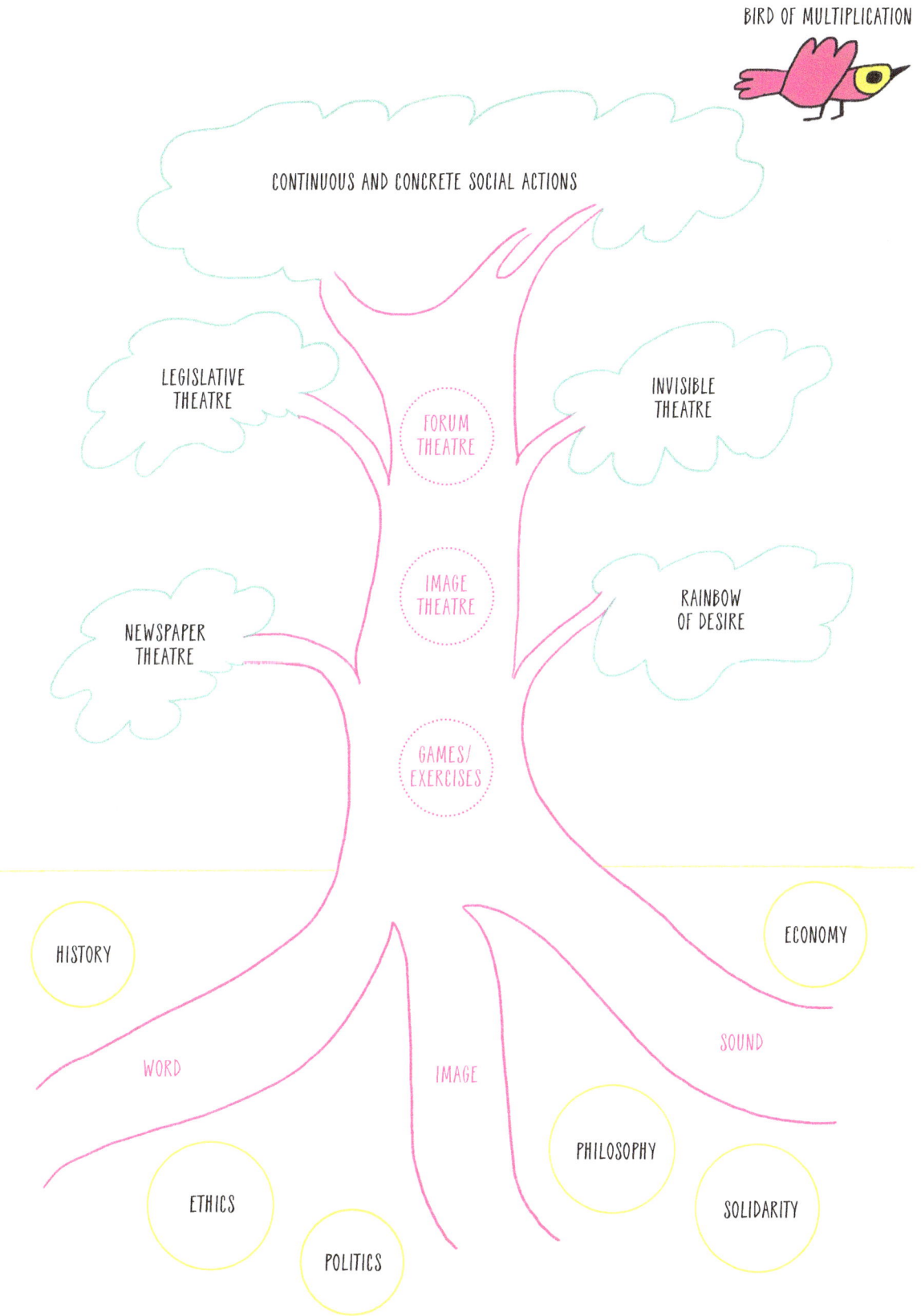

BIRD OF MULTIPLICATION

CONTINUOUS AND CONCRETE SOCIAL ACTIONS

LEGISLATIVE
THEATRE

FORUM
THEATRE

INVISIBLE
THEATRE

IMAGE
THEATRE

RAINBOW
OF DESIRE

NEWSPAPER
THEATRE

GAMES/
EXERCISES

HISTORY

ECONOMY

WORD

IMAGE

SOUND

PHILOSOPHY

ETHICS

SOLIDARITY

POLITICS

Branches of T.O. (all relating to Forum)

* RAINBOW OF DESIRE/COPS-IN-THE-HEAD
  Investigating and fighting internalized oppression, also called introspective techniques.

* INVISIBLE THEATRE
  Exposing a social problem through "guerilla theatre," in which the Spect-Actors don't know they're watching theatre.

* NEWSPAPER THEATRE
  Starting from articles in the news to develop plays.

* LEGISLATIVE THEATRE
  Inside/With a governing body, with the purpose of creating legislative proposals from the Spect-Actors' audience Interventions.

Bird of Multiplication

Our responsibility is to reproduce these tools and to use T.O. for organizing and action. This isn't just for consumption.

Continuous and Concrete Social Actions

This kind of "acting" isn't just about "reciting lines." It's about preparing to take action against oppression in our real lives.

T.O.
WEEK-BY-WEEK

Dates:

WEEK 0
Before Your First Rehearsal

* If you are doing a recruitment demo workshop, which Games will excite potential actors to join? *(Suggested: Opposite of Jackson, Forum Demo)*

_____

_____

Dates:

WEEKS 1–2
Exploration

* How will you introduce the concept of de-mechanization or good confusion? *(Suggested: Name Gumbo, Opposite of Jackson, Homage to Magritte, Great Game of Power)*

_____

_____

* How will you break the ice and build community? *(Suggested: Other name games, meditation or check-in rituals, Community Agreements)*

_____

_____

* How will you introduce key concepts (rights, systems, oppression)? *(Suggested: Anti-Oppression Lens, List possible themes via Community Needs/Human Rights discussion)*

_____

_____

*

How will you explain the process? *(Suggested: Forum Demo, Dramaturgy, T.O. Tree)*

_____

_____

Dates:

WEEKS 3-5
Creation

* How can you continue to explore de-mechanization and systemic oppression? *(Suggested: Jana Cabana, Colombian Hypnosis)*

_____

_____

_____

_____

* What Image Theatre activities will you include? *(Suggested activities: Image of the Word, Complete the Image)*

_____

_____

_____

_____

* How will you get actors to share stories and hone in on the narrative for your Forum Play? *(Suggested: Aesthetics of the Oppressed)*

_____

_____

_____

* How will you build a rough draft? *(Suggested: Scene without words)*

_____

_____

_____

_____

Dates:

WEEKS 6-8
Rehearsal

* What rehearsal Games will demechanize your current draft of the play? *(Suggested: Genre, Opera)*

_____

_____

* How can you find more details about the systems and the characters in your play? *(Suggested: Interior Monologue, Interrogation, Boxing Game, Research, Specialist Visit, Newspaper Theatre)*

_____

_____

* How will you prepare for the performance and Forum? *(Suggested: List/Make/Buy Costumes & Props; Yes, But, Pushing Against, Review Joker Flash Cards)*

_____

_____

Dates:

WEEK 9
Final Performance

* How will you warm up the actors for the show? *(Suggested activity: Meditation)*

_____

_____

_____

* How will you warm up the audience for the show? *(Suggested activities: Opposite of Jackson, Yes/No game, Image of the Word)*

_____

_____

_____

Dates:

WEEK 10
Wrap Up & Celebrate!

* How will you facilitate the troupe's celebration of themselves and each other? *(Suggested: Dancing, Paper Plate Awards)*

_____
_____
_____
_____
_____

* How will you facilitate their reflection of the process and next steps? *(Suggested: Actor Reflection Surveys)*

_____
_____
_____
_____
_____

PROJECT CHECKLISTS

**WHAT A PROJECT NEEDS /
CHECKLIST FOR YOUR PROJECT**
This is a short checklist to review the resources and information that are usually part of a theatre production. We know that people practice Theatre of the Oppressed in a wide variety of contexts. You may be working alone or coordinating a play in your school. You may be writing a grant to do a collaboration between your community group and an established theatre venue. We offer these lists so that you can think through how any item shows up in your project.

People
This is a short list of tasks and responsibilities, instead of titles, because it's highly likely that you, or people you're working with, will take on multiple responsibilities. The items on this list may be taken up by people who never step on the stage, or they may be done by actors and Jokers. Who will...?
Act.
Joker.
Coordinate everyone for rehearsals and shows.
Take notes.
Communicate with managers of the spaces you use.
Acquire, care for, and transport the materials you use, including food, props/costumes, music, printed items.
Manage the promotion of the shows.
Handle finances and payment.
Document the process with photography or video.
Communicate with donors and funders.

Resources (continued on next page)
These are things that typically support a performance, however they may not all be part of yours.
Compensation for people's work and expenses (e.g. travel stipend).
Rehearsal Space: a location where the group can meet. Consider accessibility, familiarity and comfort, ability to eat/drink and make noise.

Performance venue: Consider the same items as with your rehearsal space. Also, look for venues where Jokers and actors will be able to easily talk and interact with the audience.

Food.

Art materials, props, costumes.

Music/sound effects.

Graphic design to promote the performance.

Printing and/or Web platforms to share information with actors and the production team, show promotion, credit information.

Photography/videography, etc., to document and record the process.

Insurance. This may be required by funders or venues.

Information

Budget.

Schedule of meetings, rehearsals, performances, and celebrations.

Contact list.

PRODUCTION DESIGN AND CARE

If your play doesn't have transitions yet or you are looking for a strong beginning or ending, you can look back at any poems or songs you made to tie your scenes together. If there was an inspiration for an oversized prop or backdrop, make sure it's been created. If there are sound effects, the actors should understand how to interact with them as cues for entrances, exits, etc.

Here are some questions to ask about design choices that include care and support:

What can actors make? Are there visual artists who want to make signs?

What sound effects support the world of the play? Should you use recordings, or can actors make the sounds with their bodies, voices, props, or instruments?

Is there music that speaks to the actors' experiences?

Is there music that you play pre-show and post-show that energizes actors and brings them joy? Is anyone a DJ?

Are actors comfortable using the costumes and props that you have? Do the items fit? Are they okay to wear a hat or a wig? Do you know which items are okay to share and which aren't?

Do the costumes make actors excited?

Should we be particularly mindful with any costumes or props?

Are there costumes/props with cultural relevance, such as being sacred?

How do we treat the costumes/props represent instruments of harm, such as handcuffs, weapons, or uniforms. Do we want those items to be realistic or stylized?

Will wearing, carrying, or transporting any items put someone at risk?

PERFORMANCE-DAY CHECKLIST

On the day of the show, Jokers should wear the hat of a production stage manager. If you've never been responsible for making sure a performance happens, here's a checklist we use to make sure the actors have what they need for the show. Feel free to make changes to this template so it makes sense for your troupe's needs.

8 HOURS BEFORE SHOW

Must Dos
Call/text/email actors to remind them of the venue address and call time (when they should show up)
Confirm who is bringing props to the venue and how

Nice to Dos
Re-confirm sound operator if needed
Re-confirm food (amount, arrival, etc.)

3 HOURS BEFORE SHOW

Must Dos
Confirm tech laptop
Confirm sound operator if needed
Make sure all props are ready
Head to venue

1 HOUR 30 MINUTES BEFORE SHOW

Must Dos
Arrive at venue
Check in with venue partner
Do a sound check: make sure all the mics are working; make sure that actors can be clearly heard by the audience in different parts of the venue; run through every sound cue to check for levels (is the volume too loud/quiet?)
Make note of bathrooms in the venue; where are they? Are they gendered?
Check the food and the green room—the "backstage" area for actors
Run through stage setup
Check in with co-Joker

45 MINUTES BEFORE SHOW

Must Dos

Show the actors around the space

Make sure everyone eats something!

Confirm house open time with Front Of House (FOH), the staff or volunteer(s) who is responsible for greeting and orienting the audience to the venue

Warm up the actors

Do a walk-through of entrances, exits, cues, and bows with actors and staff

Set up an "offstage" area for actors

Nice to Dos

Introduce actors to social media person

Remind actors to stay after show to receive metro cards

Full rehearsal if there's enough time

10 MINUTES BEFORE SHOW

Must Dos

Remind actors to turn off cell phones

Tell FOH you're ready

AFTER SHOW

Must Dos

Distribute metrocards

Collect props/materials

JOKER REFLECTION ACTIVITIES

How Do I Relate to Power, Oppression, and Privilege?

This is a short exercise to offer you space to reflect on how your current perspectives may impact your Jokering. To activate your thoughts, you can play Image Theatre with the words *power, oppression, privilege.*

Power

* How do you define power?
* What are your negative connotations, what are your positive connotations?
* How comfortable are you in discussions about power?

The 4 I's of Oppression

* **Ideological.** What beliefs or ideologies do you see that are maintaining systems of oppression?
* **Institutional.** How do institutions play a role to support oppressive belief systems?
* **Interpersonal.** What do you see people do to impose these beliefs on others?
* **Internalized.** Are you aware of imposing oppressive belief systems on yourself?

Reflect on the privileges that you benefit from. Write them down.

* How easy or hard was it for you to relate The 4 I's of Oppression to what you've seen in the world? What are you curious to learn more about?
* How have your experiences informed your understanding of power?
* Is there an opportunity to leverage your privilege to support your Theatre of the Oppressed work?

WORKSHEET

Jokers Have Stories Too

Understanding the dramaturgy is great, but to facilitate this work you should have a personal connection to it. Can you describe and analyze your own story of oppression?

Looking at that story arc, think of a story from your personal life that might fit the model. Use the fill-in-the-blank prompt below if it's helpful to you:

When I was _____ *(location/time/circumstance)* _____ ,
I needed to _____ , but
_____ *(oppressor)* _____ was blocking me by
_____ because _____ .
Unfortunately, I _____ *(failure)* _____ .

You should be able to answer the following basic questions

* Who is/are the Protagonist(s)? (You should be one of them, specifically!!)
* What does the Protagonist need in this story?
* Who is/are the Antagonist(s) in this story? (There may be some invisible oppressors in this story but there should be at least one gatekeeper that the Protagonist meets.)
* What problems is the Protagonist facing in trying to get what they need?
* How does the story end?

Make Your Own T.O. Game

Much of Boal's work involved taking theatre games that he already knew and using each one as a social metaphor to open up a particular kind of dialogue. That said, we encourage you to take any exercise you are familiar with, add a facilitated debrief, and turn it into a Theatre of the Oppressed Game for de-mechanization. We love to see it.

* **Take a game that you know how to play**
(theatre game, children's game, card game, etc.)

* **What does this game remind you of?**
What might this game be a social metaphor for? (Think about power, privilege, identity or other notions we must de-mechanize.)

* **Are there new rules you can add to this game to push this metaphor further?**
Can you make the game more competitive or more challenging? What language might make the metaphor more obvious? We're looking for good confusion.

* **Play your new T.O. Game with a group**
Ask the players what their experience was and how this Game relates real life?

WORKSHEET

From Aesthetic Process to Product

Let's think about how the props, costumes, and transitions, show-promotion, or even any pre-show experience can show the size or the absurdity of the oppression.

Aesthetics of the Oppressed can relate to your marketing and audience curation! Below are some examples of figurative language that could come up in your Aesthetic Process. Use the space below to brainstorm a title and image that go along with one of these similes.

* Unemployment tastes like expired ramen.
* Childcare feels like a trap.
* This immigration paperwork looks like a mountain.
* The hospital smelled like death.
* My hood sounds like a war zone.

What about props? Can you turn these metaphors into an idea for a prop or costume that depicts the weight of the problem? Consider symbolic representations that represent institutions as well as how power might be implicated by the size, position, height, or proximity of an object.

* School is killing me.
* The police officer was a demon.

Now consider the topic of the play you are working on:

* Can props and costumes match any of the art made during the Aesthetic Process?
* Can props and costumes highlight the systems of power?

Event Self-Reflection, Accuracy/Style/Ethics

Use this worksheet after facilitating an activity.

Accuracy
* Did my instructions support the group participants in engaging in the activity I planned?
* Did anyone misunderstand my instructions? Can my guidance be clearer next time?
* What can I add to / remove from my plan that will support the intention of my activity?

Style
* What personal style did I add to set the tone for the activity?
* How did my energy seem to support people's participation?
* How did my energy seem to distract people, or lead them to participate less or not at all?

Ethics
* Did my facilitation create space to move towards liberation?

* Are people enjoying the creativity they've found with one another, perhaps in ways that oppressive systems try to shut down?
  – Are people reflecting on ways they can detach from systems that don't support them?
  – Are people acting or visioning change?

* Did I reproduce any tactics of oppressive systems or institutions?
  – Were the questions that I asked more open-ended or did I ask questions in a way that implied there was a right/wrong answer?
  – Did I show more trust or interest in people who are responding in ways I'm comfortable with?
  – Did I enforce a rule without explaining why it exists?

- Did I show or tell anyone I didn't believe them?
- Did I make space for voices that are often silenced, or did I let privileged people take up more space by default?
- What do I want to try next time?

Personal-Style Deep Dive

Here are some reflection questions that a Joker may use at regular intervals—or perhaps at the close of a project—to support self-reflection and developing flexibility. A Joker can also ask someone who has experienced or observed their facilitation for feedback.

* What are the traits of my personal expression when I facilitate? What have I been told about the energy I bring to a space?

* What are the potential impacts—positive and negative—on the specific group I am going to facilitate?

* Are there words that others use to describe my style that I feel come from bias or stereotyping, words that reflect how people see me, that are challenging for me to navigate? Do I feel offended or personally hurt when others describe my personal style?

* Can I shift the styles I use to best engage a group? How can I experiment with style so that my presence supports what I'm facilitating?

GROUP DISCUSSION TOOLS

GROUP AGREEMENT TECHNIQUES AND TEMPLATE

If your group's values include using Theatre of the Oppressed for people to connect, learn, celebrate, and support each other towards liberation, you can support the process with a Group Agreement. A Group Agreement (also called community agreement, guidelines, rules, etc.) is a tool and a practice that can communicate how the group wants to interact, support each other, and respond if there is a disagreement or problematic behavior in the space. There are many different styles and approaches to this, so we recommend you continue to explore and experiment. Here are some steps we have used in our rehearsal spaces.

1. Choose a style that fits the group

a. Predetermined: the Jokers make the community agreements themselves, without input from the participants. This style may work in a space where time is limited, and/or where participants seem resistant to identifying themselves as collaborators, and the Jokers know that they want to be transparent about what they will ask people to do, to make the rehearsal work.

b. Participant-made: the participants collaborate to generate all the agreements. This style may work in a group that is very enthusiastic about saying what they want/need (and is turned off by being told rules), or is interested in supporting their collaboration. It takes time!

c. Pre-made, with participant additions: Jokers start with some agreements, and invite the group to add what they need. This style is very similar to "participant-made," and having the facilitators start can be a tactic to model or provide momentum to the process.

2. Introduce the intent to the group

To support transparency, communicate why you are bringing a community agreement to the space.

3. Make/Establish the agreements

Facilitate a discussion about the agreements to ensure that all have been spoken in the space and clarified. Some tactics include:

a. After someone says/reads an agreement, ask someone else to describe what that means to them. Do they know other ways of saying it?

b. Check if anyone seems confused, or wants to ask a clarifying question.

4. Consent to the agreement

Once the agreements are made, how can everyone show their consent to recognize them? For example: signing a contract, thumbs up, verbal "yes"?

5. Discuss how it will be maintained in the space

Where will the agreements be displayed in the space? Is there a ritual to remind people every rehearsal or at a regular time? What should a Joker do if an individual or the group isn't keeping to an agreement? What should an actor do? (Be careful of any habits that are being used to call-out, shame, police, or exclude.) Can agreements be amended or added—when, how?

6. Are there external forces?

Is the rehearsal happening in a space that has its own rules? Do the actors already have a community agreement with each other? Does everyone know how those do or don't apply in their rehearsal?

See next page for an example of community agreements we usually offer to a new group.

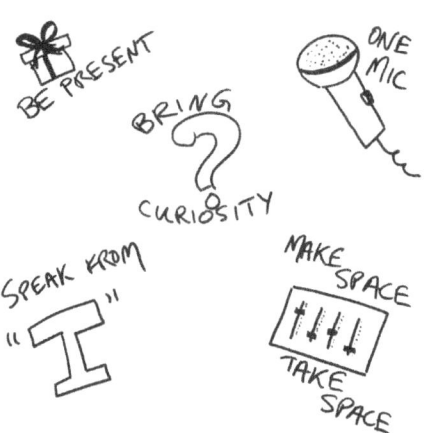

One mic

One person speaks at a time, and is given space to finish their thought, without interruption.

Be Present

We'll do what we need in order to be as present as possible and to participate, which can include putting aside unrelated activities, devices and conversations, as well as stepping out if necessary.

Speak from the "I"

To make an effort to share and reflect my own experiences, and be aware if I begin to make generalizations about others, or people like me, because then I may start speaking for someone else.

Take Space/Make Space

In order to support the value of my participation and the participation of others in the group, I must be aware how I am bringing myself to the group and adding my own perspective, while also balancing that with making space for the participation and perspective of others.

Engage Curiosity/Explore this Discomfort

Take time to be curious about things I am not familiar with or don't understand, as a step to learning and exploring how I relate to them.

ACTIVITY: ANTI-OPPRESSION LENS

While TONYC Jokers are encouraged to support the actors in the troupe in defining oppression for themselves, we do think breaking down different kinds of oppression helps actors analyze the stories they are telling. Below is TONYC's version of an exercise we learned via the Center for Racial Justice called "Lenses of Oppression." You may be familiar with a similar resource known as "The 4 I's of Oppression" (see p. 158).

We encourage Jokers who use this tool not just to define the terms below but to lean into asking actors for examples of each level of oppression to bring about a more problem-posing way of using this exercise. If you're doing it right, an argument might just break out!

Joker should draw concentric circles with:
Ideological oppression or "ism's" (outside the circle)
Joker prompt: "What are the schools of thought that provide or deny human rights based on who people think other people are (e.g., racism, sexism)?"

Institutional oppression (outermost circle)
Joker prompt: "What are the systems, institutions, policies, and practices that uphold and enact these ideologies (e.g., schools, government, etc.)?"

Interpersonal oppression (middle circle)
Joker prompt: "Think about the people impacted by those institutions. Think about the people in power who use conscious or subconscious communications and actions that take away others' rights. Let's list them. Maybe these are characters in our play! (e.g., employer-employee, doctor-patient, parent-child)?"

Internalized oppression (innermost circle)
Joker prompt: "Still considering both the oppressed and the oppressors, when the above systems are accepted consciously or subconsciously and manifest in thoughts or actions that uphold the systems of

oppression—it has been internalized. What might these characters be thinking or saying as a result of everything we've discussed? What motivates the oppressor to behave in a certain way? What stays with us when we don't get what we need? (e.g., lack of self-worth, violence needs to be punished, Immigrants are lazy, etc.)?"

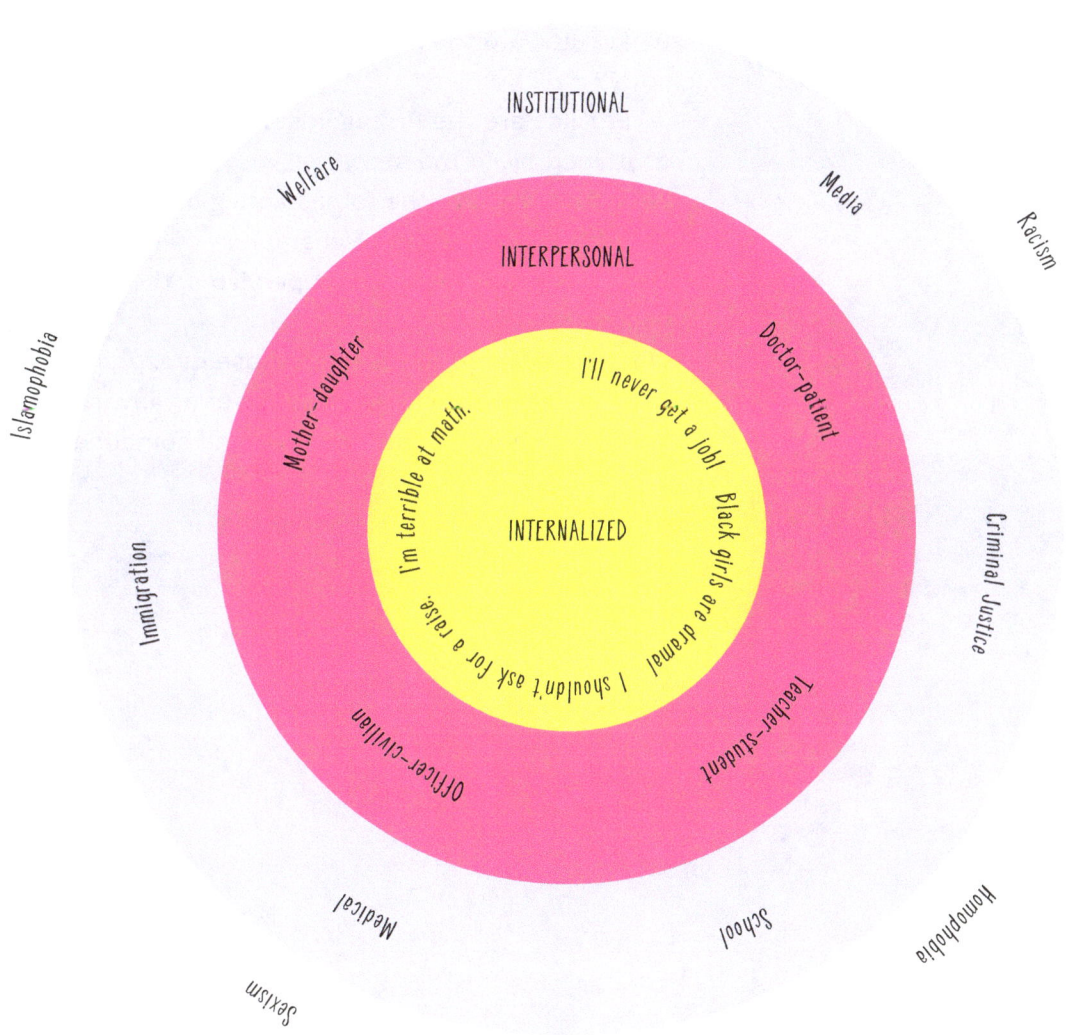

What else?

Are You Ready to Make Your Forum Play into Legislative Theatre?

At the end of rehearsals, sit down with the troupe. Have some chart paper or your notebooks and pens ready. If your troupe has a lot of answers for the following questions, consider presenting your play as a Legislative Theatre event:

* What rules are the Antagonists adhering to in the story?
* What rules are the Protagonists constricted / contained by, in the story?
* What and who are the forces acting on the Antagonists? What other characters might be in the story if we zoom-out: the supervisors, the decision makers?
* Where can we go to research these questions?
* Can we invite a social justice lawyer or advocate to our rehearsal for a chat? Can we call someone up?

DE-MECHANIZA-TION & WARM-UP GAMES

Jokers can use Games to help their actors unlearn existing social structures and norms that may be harmful to themselves and their communities.

NAME GUMBO (DE-MECHANIZATION)

For introducing the concept of "confusion"— or de-mechanization—as well as names.

1. Group Demonstration

* Two volunteers face each other and introduce themselves to each other. Freeze in handshake. Via handshake, names switch.
* Use a third volunteer to demonstrate that players continue to switch names with whomever they meet, using the last name they heard as their own.

2. Everyone plays

* Encourage the group to have fun and try and meet as many people as possible.

3. Add new instruction

* "Everyone FREEZE! Do you know the name you have right now? Continue from this point, but if your own name comes back to you, step to the side and watch.
* Make sure you give away the name you had before you leave."

* Alternate instruction
  - Let everyone reset back to having their own names.

* Continue playing
  - When most are "out" and the rest are frustrated, pause game. Ask what names are still in.

4. Debrief

* "How was that?"
(looking for: fun, confusing, weird, hard)
* "How did it feel to introduce yourself as someone

else?"

* "How did it feel to get your name back?"
* "How did it feel to not find your name?"
* "Challenges, what did people notice?"
* Introduce the "rule" of confusion: "If we aren't prepared to be a bit confused, unsure, etc., then we aren't prepared for change. We are rehearsing for the uncertainty of change."

OPPOSITE OF JACKSON (DE-MECHANIZATION)

For introducing the concept of de-mechanization, by experiencing the physical and mental challenges.

1. Demonstration

* Tell the group to walk when you say "walk" and stop when you say "stop." "Everyone walk around the room. Use the whole space. Everyone, stop!" Practice a few times. Then ask, "How is that going? Not too hard? OK, now let's make it a bit harder!"
* Tell everyone that in this Game, we will switch the meanings of words. Now, they should do the opposite of what the Joker says.

2. Everyone plays

* Now, everyone should walk when you say "stop," and stop when you say "walk. Try it out. Change up tempo, volume, attitude, etc.
* Add more pairs of words: first, describe the next pair of words with their real meanings, and practice them with the group.
  - For example, "clap" means clap and "jump" means jump.
* Practice doing the opposite briefly, playing with just the newest instructions.
* Continue playing, with all the pairs of words that you've provided so far.
* After a short time, add the next pair.
  - Tip: The Game is clearer if they are still (not moving) when they get new instructions. People may get confused about what they are supposed to be doing, if you give a new instruction while they are walking, or in motion. For instance, part of the group will clap and then keep walking, while some will stop.
* Possible instructions! We recommend selecting ones that will feel fun and accessible to the group you are playing with.
  - "Clap/Jump" (one clap and one jump).

- "Arms/Knees" (arms in the air and then down, and touch your knees and then stand).
- "Name/Yell" (say your name, short yell, "Ow!").

3. Add new instruction

* Announce that we are playing with elimination! If anyone makes a mistake, they are out of the Game.
* Tell everyone that each person will be their own judge. The Jokers will not judge who made a mistake, and the players won't judge each other.
* Ask people who are out to come to the side with you and watch the players.
* Continue the game. As people get out, challenge the people still in the game by making the instructions harder to follow.
* End the game when there's a winner, or 2-3 players remaining who can't be tricked.
* Applaud!

4. Debrief

* *"At the beginning, when you were walking when I said walk, you said it was easy. Then what happened?"*
* *"Okay, did it get harder? Why?"*
* Hear and acknowledge a range of answers. We are interested in the experience of doing what we have learned. Investigate answers that mention "instinct" or "naturally" (which suggest things that are not taught).
* Follow up to ask about sources of our learning. Try to mirror words that participants have used to challenge and question assumptions: *"Who taught us what those words mean?" "Are we programmed like computers? How can we unlearn?"*
* Connect the experience of the Game to the life experiences of the players, and what they might want to de-mechanize. "What else do we do, every day or often because... everyone else does, we are

programmed to, or people are told to do so? What programming do we want to resist? What do you do everyday that makes you itch under the skin with frustration?"

* Connect the challenge of the Game to the challenge of de-mechanizing. It takes effort, and sometimes we do what we don't want to do. "Even though you were trying to win the game, sometimes you flinched to walk when I said 'walk.'"

Notes

These pages are
yours! Feel free to
skip around, write
in the margins, rip
out pages, and add
your own ideas!

HOMAGE TO MAGRITTE (DE-MECHANIZATION)

For developing the practice of imagining radically different and creative alternatives to our current reality.

1. Demonstration to group

* Tell this story: "An artist named Magritte made a painting of an apple, and titled the painting 'This is not an apple.' He made a similar painting of a pipe. We're going to play a Game in homage to Magritte, also known as, '**This is not a water bottle**.' (You can use any everyday object in place of the water bottle, at the group's convenience: a pen, a notebook, etc.) "We will take turns using this object. You can do anything with this object except use it like a water bottle, or like the object is supposed to be used. You also can't use any words (or actually throw it, etc.). Everyone else can shout out what they think the bottle has become. If we don't understand it at first, don't tell us: add more details to your silent demonstration!"

2. Everyone plays

* Joker does a first demonstration, then the participants play. After each improvisation with a water bottle the group shouts out what they see. The game can go around the circle, or in a random order. Everyone is encouraged to take a turn, or more than one turn if they're inspired.

3. Add new instruction

* Now do the same, but make the object a bit bigger or more challenging: for example, "This is not a chair." We have to transform the chair into something totally new, again without words.

4. Debrief

* *"Why do you think Magritte painted a painting of a pipe and titled it 'This is not a pipe?'"*

* *"What did we need to do to play this Game?"*
  Looking for responses which could include:
  - Seeing things as other than what they are.
  - Activating the radical imagination: if we can imagine things as other than they are, we can reimagine those things that are oppressive, and change them.
  - Nonverbal communication—i.e., using images— allows us to communicate with each other much more quickly and precisely and across some cultural divides. This can help identify our collective struggle and then reimagine it.

* *"Finally, we are already making theatre with what we have, with the skills we have. We performed, and our audience saw and understood. We have everything we need to do this work as both activists and artists".*

JANA CABANA (DE-MECHANIZATION)

For silliness, fun, competition, and collaboration.

1. Demonstration to a group

* Ask for three volunteers to demonstrate:
  - Instruct 2 volunteers to make a "House" by facing each other and raising their arms so that palms meet to form an angled roof. Ask the third volunteer to be the Person inside the House—that is, slightly crouched down between/under two people who have formed a House.
* Tell the group that there are three commands that anyone who is "out" can say: "House, People, and Storm."
* Use yourself as the person who is out. With your volunteers, show that if you call "People," all those crouching in Houses have to leave and quickly run to occupy another House. The Houses stay in place. Then someone else will be "out." If you call "House," the people making the house must break apart and find a new Person to form a House over (the People stay in place). If you say "Storm," everyone must become either a House, or a Person under a House, in order to not be left out.

2. Everyone plays

* Ask everyone to make Houses occupied by People throughout the space. One participant is out.
* The person who is out gets to call either House, People, or Storm, and then tries to get back into the Game, leaving another person out.
* Clarify instructions if folks are confused. You may need to repeat the instructions a few times throughout the Game. Remind everyone to keep the Houses spread out if it gets too crowded.

3. Debrief

* *"What did you notice about yourself as you participated in this activity? What did you notice*

about the group?"

* *"What strategies did you use to find a new trio?"*
* *"What connections can we make between this strategy and strategies to make change or survive oppression?"* (Looking for conversations about basic needs and group problem solving.)

COLOMBIAN HYPNOSIS (DE-MECHANIZATION)

For de-mechanizing the body and examining interpersonal and systemic power relationships.

1. Demonstration

* Ask for two volunteers: one is person A, the other is person B. This is a completely nonverbal activity.
* First, A puts their hand, palm facing out, about 8 inches away from person B's face, with the base of the palm roughly in line with B's chin. "A" moves hand, verrrrryyyy slowly at first, so that B can follow with their face and then their whole body.
  - The idea is that the distance between A's hand and B's face should stay the same throughout, and it is everyone's responsibility to keep the same distance. "A" always moves slowly, carefully, so that their hand can be followed.
  - They may try different kinds of movements once a relationship has been established and they get a sense of B's ability to follow.
* Then after a few minutes of exploration, while continuing to move slowly and seamlessly, "B" raises their hand and "B" and "A" switch roles. Continue.
* After a few minutes, "B" keeps their hand up, and "A" raises their hand again, so that both partners are leading and both are following simultaneously.
* At some point, the Joker asks the volunteers to freeze in the next 30 seconds, on their own time.

2. Everyone plays

* Everyone in pairs, all at the same time. Before starting, they can ask if the other person has any injuries / movement boundaries they want to share.
* Whoever is leading needs to keep an eye on others moving around the space as well, to avoid collisions.
* Joker calls out timings to switch leaders gracefully from A to B, and then move to both leading / following together.
* At the end, come to a rest in some position without speaking. Relax.

3. Add new instruction/variation. The whole group follows one "leader" (no longer in pairs)

* **Demonstration for new setup**
  - One volunteer stands in the center of the circle. That person begins moving all their limbs slowly, with their feet planted.
  - Another volunteer from the circle steps in to begin following a body part of the first leader: perhaps their hand, or knee, or elbow, or hip, etc.

* **Everyone plays**
  - Then slowly, more people from the circle step in, each following a different body part of any person in the circle, while also allowing their own limbs to move slowly. (Make sure that the followers stay distanced enough from the leader to maintain personal safety and comfort.)
  - Once the majority of the group is following someone else in the center, the Joker can ask all the followers to move out slowly, continuing to follow the person they're watching while creating more distance between them, and then move back in slowly.

4. Debrief

* *"How was it?" (challenges, fun?)*
* *"Did anyone prefer being leader or follower? Why?"*
* *"How did it feel to be following and leading at the same time? How did you navigate that?"*
* In the final full-group variation: *"How did it feel when everyone was following one person in the center? Did that remind you of any relationships or dynamics in the world around us?"*
* Guide conversation towards: Physical de-mechanization; Power dynamics challenging your partner physically, so they are in different positions than in everyday life.

GREAT GAME OF POWER (DE-MECHANIZATION)

For revealing people's understanding of how power works.

1. Demonstration

* Place 3 chairs (all the same) in a row, in front of the group.
* Ask for a volunteer to silently arrange the chairs in such a way that, in their opinion, 1 chair has more power than all the other chairs.
* Join the audience and wait for the volunteer to arrange the chairs.
* Once the chairs have been arranged, ask that volunteer to return to their seat and not reveal their thinking behind the arrangement.

2. Everyone plays

* Ask the group to interpret or "read" the image made by the chairs. "What do you see?"
* Invite the group to analyze their interpretation. "Why do you say that? What is another interpretation of this position? Which chair has the most power? Why?"
* Support different interpretations, as information about how people in the room see, experience, and imagine power. The volunteer might get frustrated that people aren't understanding their intentions. Encourage them to make space for new interpretations that might expand everyone's understanding of power.
* At the end of the discussion (if it hasn't already been said), invite the volunteer to share their intentions.

3. Add new instruction

* Ask for another volunteer to move the chairs into a new arrangement.
* Facilitate the same discussion to hear people's interpretations.
* If you play three or more rounds, add variation:
  - Volunteer can use 3 chairs and a water bottle.
  - Volunteer can add themselves to the sculpture of chairs.

– After discussing an example, invite each participant to add themselves one by one, and each new person is trying to be in a position that makes them the most powerful.

4. Debrief

* *"Did you notice any themes about power, or commonly-held beliefs about power, that came up in our examples and reflections? For example, we often associate a central or elevated position as 'the most powerful.'"*
* Investigate any moments when people debated interpretations, and connect the tension to the world around us. For example, if someone has stacked chairs, some will say that the top chair is most powerful, and others will point out that the bottom chair is holding it up. This is a great metaphor for workers and CEOs, etc. The group may also bring up the difference between oppressive power and collective power.
* If you are already building scenes: *"Think about how physical relationships can be used to highlight the power dynamics in the scene."*

FORUM SCENE DEMONSTRATION

THE HANDSHAKE FORUM AND THE MARCHERS FORUM (FORUM SCENE DEMOS)

For introducing a group to the way Forum Theatre works, and for guiding the scene-building.

1. Demonstration

* Tell the group that you are going to perform a short Forum scene. Ask for volunteer(s) to act with you.
* Here are two scenarios we use in demonstrations: the Handshake Forum and the Marcher's Forum. For the Handshake Forum, you will need 1 volunteer. For Marcher's Forum, ask for 4-5.
* Welcome the volunteer(s) and tell them what to do in the scene. They are not allowed to use words.
  - **For Handshake Forum.** Tell the volunteer that you will stand on opposite sides of the room, walk towards each other, and shake hands. All the volunteer needs to know about their character is that they need to get a handshake. (The volunteer is the scene's Protagonist, and you are the Antagonist.)
  - **For the Marcher's Forum.** Tell the group that they live in a world where they must march together from one side of the room to another, and must keep marching at all costs. Take one person aside, and tell them to eventually start skipping or dancing. (The skipper is the scene's Protagonist.)

2. Everyone Plays

* Ask the volunteers if they are ready. Once they are, ask the audience to say "3, 2, 1, action!"
  - **For Handshake Forum.** Walk towards your volunteer scene partner as if to shake hands, hand extended, smiling, but at the last minute don't shake, and cross your arms. Use your body and expression to show that you are the person in power. Let the volunteer actor react and perhaps try to get the handshake 1-2 other ways.
  - **For Marcher's Forum.** Watch the scene. Make sure that the volunteer remembers the secret

instruction to skip instead of march. Let the other actors react, and perhaps try to make the skipper return to marching.

* After not too long, say "scene" to end the acting, and start applause. Thank the actors, and ask them to stay with you while you ask the audience some questions.

3. Engage the audience to be Spect-Actors

* Ask audience: "What happened?" Get information on how the characters interacted, highlighting the attempts to change other characters. Ask: "What did the Protagonist(s) need?" In the Handshake Forum, the Protagonist was trying to get the handshake, respect. In the Marcher's Forum, the skipper was trying to move freely but the group was trying to control them.

* "Have you ever been in that character's shoes? How does that feel?"
    - **For Handshake Forum.** "Have you ever tried to get someone to acknowledge you and they refused or ignored you?"
    - **For Marcher's Forum.** "Have you ever tried to do your own thing, and other people tried to get you to conform?"

* "So now, this character is not alone. You've been there too and you know this sucks. Does anyone want to come up and replay the scene but try something different to get what you need?"

* If someone volunteers, they should tap out the actor who is the scene's "Protagonist" and then replay the scene from the start. The new volunteer is allowed to try something new this time. Other actors will respond to what they try. "We are inviting you to do this because we believe this situation can change and hope you do too even if it's difficult! Remember, no talking!"

* Start the scene with "3, 2, 1, action!"

* Stop the scene with applause once we've seen their idea play out.

* Thank the most recent volunteer and let them sit down.

* Ask the Spect-Actors: "What did they try? What happened? How did it change the Antagonist(s)? Would this strategy be possible for everyone? What might be the pitfalls of this idea? What might happen next?"
* Ask for another volunteer who wants to try something different. Replay the scene and repeat the debrief questions.
* Try to do at least 3 ideas. Note: we're not looking for the best idea; we're trying ideas and seeing what happens.

4. Debrief

* You can say something like: "The situation in this scene is a stand-in for the experience of trying to access a human or community right, and getting blocked. We use a Forum Scene to show you a problem. You identify the problem, then try out ideas to attempt to change the situation. That is Forum Theatre. Instead of a handshake/skipping, the scene could be about trying to get housing, or confronting discrimination."
* "When we make a Forum Scene, it is based on the real-life experiences of the people performing." (Tell the story of Boal and the farmer, and how Boal began to follow Freire's ethics that the people experiencing the problem must be at the center of changing it.)
* "The Forum is a rehearsal for real life, and it actually is real life, because it's a real problem, and we are the ones trying new alternatives in real time."
* "It's different from giving advice. If we get up because we've been in that situation and/or we want it to change, we are rehearsing an idea for ourselves, and showing it to everyone else."
* This is a strong moment to ask the group what kind of problems they would make a play about, or to build a list of themes (needs or rights of this community or group).

Notes

These pages are
yours! Feel free to
skip around, write
in the margins, and
rip out pages, and
add your own ideas!

IMAGE THEATRE ACTIVITIES

Jokers can use Image Theatre activities like the ones below to get comfortable using their body and facial expressions to articulate emotions and power dynamics.

IMAGE OF THE WORD (Image Theatre)

For practicing physical storytelling and identifying the group's connection to specific themes for solidarity building.

1. Demonstration

* Participants make a big circle, facing out. Say, "When I say a word or phrase, build your body into a sculpture/image of that word, using facial expressions as well as your full range of movement." After everyone has had a chance to build their sculpture, count "1, 2, 3, Image," and everyone turns around to face in and see all the images. (Participants may re-create their image after turning around or attempt to stay in their image while turning.)

2. Everyone plays

* Start with warm-up words that are lighter in theme: birthday, beach, or maybe the city you're in (e.g., New York). Move on to themes that have come up in rehearsal: education, health care, social worker, etc. While everyone holds their image, invite everyone to say out loud the things they see around the circle. This can be feelings, gestures, or ideas: "Anger." "Bored." "Arms closed, protective." "Mean teacher."

3. Add additional instructions / variations (use one or all of these)

* **Families.** Say, "While holding your image, move into a 'family,' a group of other images that fit with yours." Like before, each group can look at the other families one by one and talk about what they see. These families can turn into story-sharing groups on a specific topic pretty seamlessly.
* **Repeated elements.** Individuals can add a sound, speak a word, or make a repetitive movement for

their image.

* **Dubbing.** Invite one participant to step in and give voice to what another person's image/character is saying/thinking.

4. Debrief

* *"Was anything surprising about these words/topics as they became embodied?"*

* *"Did you find any alignment or solidarity within your 'families' as you began to tell stories? What might that tell us about the power of nonverbal communication?"*

A word about Image Theatre "debriefs"

Image Theatre exercises are different than de-mechanization Games, in that they aim to get actors more comfortable with physical storytelling without words. Feel empowered to keep these conversations on the shorter side and use the momentum of actors being on their feet to get to the next image or draft of the scene. Maybe you reflect at the very end of rehearsal instead of directly after the exercise. (Brush up on your understanding of Image Theatre by going back to p. 40)

COMPLETE THE IMAGE (Image Theatre)

For strengthening our ability to create relationships between characters and analyze power dynamics.

1. Demonstration

* Ask two volunteers to face each other in the "stage" area. They shake hands, and then the Joker calls, "Freeze!" The volunteers become statues, frozen in the moment of a handshake.
* Joker asks the rest of the group: "What do you see here?" People may say, "I see two friends" or "I see two enemies" or "I see a business deal." Joker asks: "Why do you see that? What specifically is giving you the impression that they're friends or enemies?" Someone may answer: "That person's raised eyebrow suggests anger," or "This person is leaning forward, which suggests more power."
* Now, person #1 steps out of the picture (while person #2 stays frozen!), and #1 makes a new pose, to "complete the image" in a totally new way. Thus, #2 still has their hand extended like half a handshake, but #1 may be crouching, lying on the ground, raising a fist in the air, or whatever they choose.
* Then we analyze it again. "Now what do you see?"
* Next, person #2 (who had been frozen) steps out of their pose, and completes the image in a totally new way... and so on.

2. Everyone plays

Everyone forms pairs to play the game at the same time. Identify who is #1 and who is #2, so that the pair knows who will unfreeze to "complete the image" first. Then start from a frozen handshake.

3. Add new instructions / variations

* Joker freezes one pair and the rest can relax and watch them work, alternating between frozen images and changing the image. The Joker then pauses the pair on an image that is particularly

compelling or gets a big reaction. It may be an image that evokes a power relationship, or a conflict. Then, the group analyzes the image.

* **Dubbing**. While the group is looking at a frozen image, an observer can approach one of the frozen images and put their hand on or near the actor's shoulder, saying what they believe the character could be saying or thinking. One "dubber" can dub both people in the image, or just one character at a time.

   Zoom out. When the group is analyzing a frozen pair,
* they may suggest a scenario that could involve other characters. For example, if someone in the group calls out that they see "a fight in the schoolyard," the Joker can ask: "What other characters could be in this scene, in this one moment? Let's zoom out like a camera lens to see more of the story." Then other group members can add themselves one by one into the frozen image, without speaking, pretending to be other characters in the scene— the teachers, other peers, etc. Joker can then add "dubbing" so that other participants can speak the imagined lines of the characters in the image.

4. Debrief

"What did you notice? What struck you as we were
* *playing?"*

Looking for:

- It's so easy to create stories (as we move towards making a play).
- We project stories onto images from our individual and shared experiences.
- There can be multiple perspectives about one image, and all of those can hold some truth.
- Subjective versus Objective. As in, one person sees a narrative in an image based on their experience of the world which could be seen differently by someone else (subjective); versus the undeniable facts about what we're all looking at (objective). This is useful for analyzing situations of oppression later in a Forum process.

SCENE WITHOUT WORDS / ROUGH DRAFT OF STORY

(IMAGE THEATRE)

To draft scenes quickly that are rooted in strong physical choices.

1. Demonstration

* Prompt actors to make a short performance, without words, to convey the story and problem. Encourage them not to sit and plan too much. Try it. Rehearse. The goal is to make the story as clear as possible and fit the structure of the Forum Play.

2. Watch the scenes (You do not need to give the viewers any context for the story.)

3. Debrief

* Viewers debrief, while actors who created the scene just listen:

"What do we understand?"
– "Who is the Protagonist?"
– "What do they need?"
– "Did we see the problem?"
– "What might these characters be saying?"
– "Anything we want to know more about?"
–

Notes

These pages are
yours! Feel free to
skip around, write
in the margins, and
rip out pages, and
add your own ideas!

AESTHETICS OF THE OPPRESSED ACTIVITIES

Jokers can use the Aesthetics of the Oppressed to support actors in creating poems, paintings, sculptures, music, and even comedy gags to express emotional experiences that may be difficult to communicate verbally.

AESTHETICS OF THE OPPRESSED

For exploring and communicating the emotional content of our scenes. For building solidarity among actors.

1. Demonstration/Setting up

* Create three mini-teams per Forum scene. (If you have multiple groups making scenes, each scene group will break into three smaller teams.) Each mini-team is comprised of 1-2 people who will work together on a small project within a specific artistic medium. The teams may be as follows:
  - Sculpture.
  - 2D Art.
  - Poetry.
* Encourage people to choose a medium that they don't necessarily feel "good" or skilled at.
* Each mini-team will be using their medium to show the feeling of the problem in their scene. This can be abstract. They should not make a literal representation of the situation or try to tell the story.
* Participants may talk to the other person they are collaborating with on their mini-team but the mini-teams cannot talk to the other teams during the art-making, even if they are using the same scene for inspiration.
* Provide participants with appropriate materials and guidelines:
  - **2-dimensional (2D) art.** Use flat paper, markers, crayons, pens, pencils, magazines for collage, etc. They should not include any words or symbols in their art.
  - **Sculpture.** Use scissors, tape, glue, and a collection of "clean trash." These are items that would

typically be discarded or recycled, like boxes, wrapping paper, broken objects, etc. Anything that the Jokers or participants gathered, as long as it is clean. They should not include words.

- **Poetry.** Use paper and pens/pencils. Poetry can also mean song or rap.

Give everyone 15-20 minutes to make something.

2. Everyone Plays

* If groups are spending more than 5 minutes talking about what they will do, nudge them to begin making.

* Let everyone know when they have 5 minutes left.

* Support people with any questions. But if they are using questions or perfectionism as a way to avoid diving in, gently push them towards doing. You can say, "Whatever you think I just said, go for it!"

3. Debrief Part 1: Guide the tour/aesthetics exhibit

* View each story's three pieces, one at a time (order below) with the following guidelines:

- **Rules.** The group working on the scene/story to which the art belongs CANNOT SPEAK (they listen and can take notes that connect to their scene-building). It's best if they stand behind the audience.

- **Intentions.** We are seeking to understand the way Aesthetics can convey the emotional content and urgency of the piece, not necessarily the details of the story. This art helps us to invest in the story through making art together—create a vibe.

- **Solidarity.** When we take away the narrative details we can focus on the elements of the story that connect to human emotion and motivate change.

* First, view: Sculpture/Clean Trash

- Remind everyone, "We are thinking about how the problem in the scene feels. We don't have to guess what the story is."

- Participants offer objective observations and subjective interpretations for each work of art. For example, a participant might say, "I see anger."

(Joker asks, "Why/where do you see anger?") Participant continues, "Because there's a lot of red paper..."

* Second, add 2D art in front of sculpture: 2D art is now the spotlight of the discussion.
  - Ask, "What more do we see?"
  - Looking for: new information and connections, continuing with subjective and objective commentary.
* Third, add poetry
  - Those who wrote the poem(s) stand behind viewers, who continue looking at 2D art and sculpture. (They perform the poetry slowly and audibly.)
  - Ask, "What words or images stood out to you? What do you feel or understand now?"
* Give applause for all mini-teams. If you have multiple scene groups, repeat the viewing of sculpture, art, and poetry for each scene.

4. Final Debrief

* Ask everyone to reflect on how the art connected them. If people said, "We didn't even talk about it, but our art had the same things going on in it," connect that to how their shared experiences show up in their scene.
* Talk about how the emotional content and impact of their art is important to bring to their scene. The Spect-Actors will be motivated if the scene makes them understand how the problem feels. Emotions are an important part of the experience, and can be represented creatively and abstractly when they are performing.

REHEARSAL GAMES

Jokers can use rehearsal Games to help actors explore and know their characters and their circumstances more deeply.

BOXING ACTIVITY (REHEARSAL GAMES)

To prepare actors to be verbally strong and responsive as Antagonists. The Game can also help actors prepare for difficult real-life encounters, like self-advocacy at a medical or benefits appointment, or activism.

1. Demonstration

* Ask for a volunteer who feels confident in speaking the beliefs of the Antagonist in the Forum Scene. Ask that person to stand in the middle of the room.
* Instruct everyone else to stand around the space, forming a boxing ring, with the first volunteer on one side of it.
* Tell the group that there is an imaginary line in the middle of the ring, which the Antagonist cannot cross.
* When the Game begins, the Antagonist will give a short speech that summarizes their character's main points. This is how they argue the "right-ness" of the oppression. It is like the first blow in the fight.
* After the first blow, anyone can step into the other side of the ring and give a counterargument. The Antagonist has to listen and then retort. They will continue to exchange arguments.
* When other participants see either player losing, they can stand behind that person, wait until they are not speaking, then tap them out and replace them. The debate continues without a pause.

2. Everyone plays

* Anyone in the ring can step in for either player. There are no teams. The Game is to bring full arguments to both sides.
* You can support the flow of the Game, by allowing people to line up behind someone if they hear

fundamental flaws that will eventually weaken their argument.

* Do not allow players to replace someone who is winning, even if they think they can win it. It's not about winning; it's about keeping the dialogue (i.e., the drama) going.
* Cheerlead if needed!
* Stop the Game based on time or energy.

3. Debrief

* Offer a moment to shake off the debate. People might need a moment to tell the group that the words in their argument aren't what they believe. People may need recognition for voicing and fighting oppression.
* *"Did you hear or see anything that could be used by the scene's actors to deepen the scene?"*
* *"What tactics did you use to keep bringing arguments to the debate?"* Connect those tactics to the work of improvising with Spect-Actors.

PUSHING AGAINST ONE ANOTHER (REHEARSAL GAMES)

To prepare actors to improvise with Spect-Actors, by remembering to listen and respond to their ideas.

1. Demonstration

* Ask for 2 volunteers, or demonstrate yourself with a partner.
* The people demonstrating face each other, put their palms together, and imagine a line on the floor between them (under where their hands meet). While
* playing, they are supposed to push against their partner as hard as possible, but only as hard as their partner pushes back. They are striving to win, but also collaborating to stay in the Game (instead of pushing each other over the line).
* Ask the people demonstrating to keep playing, but with less force. Then add force. Point out that each partner has to feel and respond.
* Stop the demonstration.

2. Everyone plays

* Ask people to pair up. If people are concerned about strength or height, remind them that the Game is about responding to match your partner.
* Play.
* Pause the Game after a brief time.

3. Debrief

* Connect the responsiveness of the Game to the task of improvising with a Spect-Actor. During the Forum, Spect-Actors will 'push against' the scene, especially the oppression in it. In order for the Joker, actors, and audience to understand their idea, the actors need to make space to hear what they are trying to do, and then respond realistically, and with enough 'force' to allow the idea to develop. If the actors give in, and let the Spect-Actor's idea 'win' easily, does

this mean that the oppression in the scene can be overcome that easily? If the actors try to win without hearing the idea, does the oppression seem so powerful that no other Spect-Actor wants to try?

* Guide discussion towards:
  - Training the Antagonist to be strong but listen.
  - Reminding actors that they are playing the character and to be aware of how the improvisation is going.
  - Figuring out what this character really would say and do in every scenario.
  - Listening for the Spect-Actor's new idea.

INTERIOR MONOLOGUE AND INTERROGATION (REHEARSAL GAMES)

These are two Games that can be played separately or together

For deepening the actors' understanding of their characters' feelings and thoughts and for highlighting the systems of oppression that lie beneath the characters' actions and words.

1a. Demonstration

* Set the scene from the top, and instruct all characters to speak their interior monologue aloud before the scene begins. *Interior monologue* means the thoughts and feelings that the character might not say out loud during the scene. It can also be described as the "stream of consciousness" of the character.

2a. Everyone plays

* The characters must all speak their interior monologue without stopping, while the rest of the group walks around and listens.

3a. Transition to INTERROGATION

* Say something to the actors like: "Whatever you learned about your characters' feelings, needs, and motivations can inform the dialogue and the action for the next run-through." When the Joker calls "GO" to start the scene, the audience sits down.

1b. Demonstration

* The actors immediately start their scene or play from the beginning.
* The audience, i.e., the rest of the group that's not in this particular scene, can raise their hands at any point during the action to ask probing questions of the characters. These might include, "Mom character, what are you really thinking?" "Doctor, why don't you believe your patient?" and other questions about what the characters believe and why

they act the way they do. These are not questions for the actors. They are for the characters!

* When at least three audience members have raised their hands, Joker calls out, "Pause" and calls on audience members to ask their questions.

2b. Everyone plays

* We raise our hand to pause the scene to ask characters probing and revealing questions. Actors stay in character as they answer audience questions (and when we go back into the scene).
* Let the audience ask a few questions each time you stop, and then call "Action!" again to restart the scene. Work through the whole scene in this way.

3c. Debrief

* *"What did you discover about the characters in these two Games?"*
* Actors can incorporate the discoveries as we continue to refine the scene.

OPERA (REHEARSAL GAMES)

For heightening the expression of the problem and its impact on the characters in the play, and for creating some levity in the rehearsal process.

1. Demonstration

* Tell the group that we're going to play the scene, but the Joker will call out an emotion, and everyone plays out the action of the scene with that heightened, exaggerated emotion. This is called "Opera" because in an opera, all the emotions are way over the top.
* It's important to remember that the action and essential dialogue won't change, even if the emotion contradicts the dialogue!

2. Everyone plays

* Joker calls out an emotion to start, and after a few minutes in the scene with all characters playing that exaggerated emotion, they call out a new emotion and the action continues. These may include: Happy, sad, angry, loving, jealous, bored, scared, excited, giggly, flirty, etc.
* Audience / other group members can suggest emotions that might heighten a particular moment or contradict it entirely.
* Joker should keep encouraging actors to heighten the emotions—play them over the top!
* Continue playing to the end of the scene or until everyone is exhausted.

3. Debrief

* Ask the audience (that is, the rest of the group):
  - *"When was the emotion really appropriate and highlighted something we didn't previously know about the scene?"*
  - *"Which moments from the game should we keep* (for example, everyone laughing hilariously after the judge gives the sentence, or erupting into anger after slamming the door to the house, etc)?"

GENRE (REHEARSAL GAMES)

For heightening the expression of the problem and its impact on the characters in the play, and for creating some levity in the rehearsal process.

1. Demonstration

* This is very similar to the Opera rehearsal Game. Tell the group that we're going to play the scene, but the Joker will call out a genre, and everyone plays out the action of the scene in the style of that genre.
* Ask the group to name some genres, so we get an idea of what that might include.
* It's important to remember that the action and essential dialogue won't change, even if the genre contradicts the dialogue!

2. Everyone plays

* Joker calls out a genre to start, and after a few minutes in the scene with all characters playing that exaggerated genre, the Joker calls out a new genre and the action continues. These may include: ballet, soap opera, children's show, detective movie, action movie.
* Audience / other group members can suggest genres that might heighten a particular moment or contradict it entirely.
* Joker should keep encouraging actors to play the genres over the top!
* Continue playing to the end of the scene or until everyone is exhausted.

3. Debrief

* Ask the audience (that is, the rest of the group):
  - *"When did the genre highlight something we didn't previously know about the scene?"*
  - *"Which moments should we keep from this Game (for example, entering the doctor's office as in a horror movie)?"*

RESOURCES FOR FURTHER READING

At TONYC, we turn to the following kinds of resources to supplement our work:

* Anti-racism trainings.
* Trauma-informed material.
* Restorative justice tools.

Pedagogy and Theatre of the Oppressed resources

* *Pedagogy of the Oppressed* by Paulo Freire
* *Games for Actors and Non-Actors* by Augusto Boal
* *Theatre of the Oppressed* by Augusto Boal
* *Theatre of the Oppressed: Roots and Wings* by Bárbara Santos
* *Teaching to Transgress* by bell hooks
* *Rainbow of Desires Study Materials* by MTÜ Foorumteater and VAT Teatri Foorumgrupp, available online at https://issuu.com/nikolaikunitson/docs/rod_eng
* *An A to Z of Theory | Augusto Boal: Aesthetics and Human Becoming* by Andy McLaverty-Robinson, available at https://ceasefiremagazine.co.uk/augusto-boal-aesthetics-human/

Other resources

* www.trainingforchange.org
* www.transformharm.org

ACKNOWLEDG-
MENTS

This publication was co-authored by **Theatre of the Oppressed NYC (TONYC)** staff members Sulu LeoNimm and Liz Morgan with TONYC founder and former executive director Katy Rubin. Other TONYC staff, Jokers, actors, and volunteers collaborated on testing this workbook and contributed stories and narrative to the document. This work would not be possible without the countless community members who gave their time and talents to TONYC's Forum Theatre residencies and workshops; see credits (p. 208) for more.

TONYC collaborated with Fielding Hong, Siyona Ravi, Marisa Hetzler, and Yasmin Safdie from the **Center for Urban Pedagogy (CUP),** and illustrator-designers Shreyas R Krishnan and Kruttika Susarla. CUP has been a longtime partner and source of inspiration for TONYC, so it was a joy to work together on the structure, illustrations, and design for this handbook.

CREDITS

The **CENTER FOR URBAN PEDAGOGY (CUP) is** a nonprofit organization that uses the power of design and art to increase meaningful civic engagement, in partnership with historically marginalized communities. *welcometocup.org*

THEATRE OF THE OPPRESSED NYC
partners with community members at local organizations to form theatre troupes. These troupes devise and perform plays based on their challenges confronting economic inequality, racism, and other social, health and human rights injustices. After each performance, actors and audiences engage in theatrical brainstorming – called Forum Theatre – with the aim of catalyzing creative change on the individual, community, and political levels. *tonyc.nyc*

SAME SAME BUT DIFFERENT is Shreyas R Krishnan and Kruttika Susarla—illustrator-designers from Tamil Nadu and Andhra Pradesh. They are both interested in visual culture, and work collaboratively on comics, zines, and posters. *samesamebutdifferent.work*

CUP: Fielding Hong, Siyona Ravi, Marisa Hetzler, Yasmin Safdie

TONYC: Liz Morgan (project manager) with Sulu LeoNimm & Katy Rubin

Same Same But Different: Shreyas R Krishnan and Kruttika Susarla

Big thanks to all the TONYC staff and community members who shared stories and feedback especially Amorarey Sandoz, Julian Pimiento, Lovely Penny Bonhomme, Titus Battle, Darryl Campbell, Katie Diamond, Meggan Gomez, Omari Soulfinger, Philip Santos Schaffer, Letitia Bouie, Mike Gonzalez, Spark LeoNimm, Maaji Nishizaka, Stan Benes, Réka Polonyi and Micah Bucey

Support for this project was provided by a grant from the New York Community Trust *nycommunitytrust.org*

Copyright © 2022 by Theatre of the Oppressed NYC

www.ingramcontent.com/pod-product-compliance
Lightning Source LLC
Chambersburg PA
CBHW080129150626

46550CB00018B/2928